Avoiding
The Danger Zone
Business Illusions

By

Jerry L. Mills, CPA

Avoiding The Danger Zone, Business Illusions

www.avoidingthedangerzone.com

Library of Congress Cataloging-in-Publication Data
is available upon request.

ISBN 0-9800349-0-5

First Edition, November 2007

Name Changes

Some case-study names have been changed

Acknowledgement

The partners of **B2B CFO**®

Contents

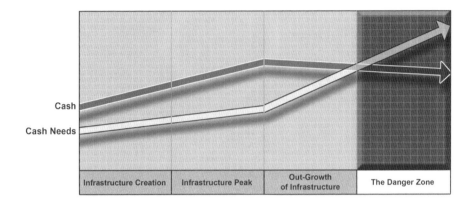

Cash				
Cash Needs				
	Infrastructure Creation	Infrastructure Peak	Out-Growth of Infrastructure	The Danger Zone

INTRODUCTION

My book, The Danger Zone, Lost in the Growth Transition, defined **The Danger Zone** as the situation wherein the cash needs of a company far exceed the available cash. This situation often causes a Chapter 11 bankruptcy filing, liquidation of assets or other time-consuming planning events in order to salvage the company.

The past 30 years have taught me much about how business owners react to both avoid and escape The Danger Zone. I have witnessed first-hand the business conditions of more than 100 companies during my career. Consequently, I have realized for some time that it might be beneficial to other business owners to read about some of the experiences I have witnessed.

Much has been written about the stories of Fortune 100/500 companies as they have gone through their business cycles of success or failure. While their stories are interesting, it is often difficult for the owners of closely-held businesses to

1

relate to the business problems of companies that are doing billions of dollars in annual sales.

BUSINESS EMPLOYMENT

Non-Fortune 100/500 businesses employ the majority of the employees in our nation. A February 2007 article states:

> According to the U.S. Small Business Administration, there are around 25.8 million businesses in the United States with 100 or fewer employees. These companies generated between 60 and 80 percent of the new jobs created annually over the past decade. Collectively, they are a significant driver of the U.S. economy.[1]

The combination of Moore's Law and other economic factors will cause an increase in the number of these businesses in the future, hence the importance to address their needs and concerns.

RESPECT

The partners of my firm refer to the businesses described above by the U.S. Small Business Administration as entrepreneurial, growth or mid-market companies.

I hold the owners of such companies in the highest respect. Many have become my heroes. Such owners are usually not only risk-takers but are bright, articulate and creative. Most have work ethics and values that put the rest of our society to shame. It has been my privilege to work with some of the brightest and best of our business society.

I truly admire the risk-taking attributes of these entrepreneurs. A CEO of a Fortune 500 company who makes errors can get fired but often leaves the company with millions of dollars in cash or stock options. Conversely, the CEO of a growth or mid-market company who makes errors can literally lose everything — the company, personal assets and close personal relationships.

BUSINESS ILLUSIONS

The majority of this book consists of stories of actual situations in which I have been involved during my career. Not only are the stories interesting, but there is much to learn from each situation. The cumulative knowledge that can be gained from all of these stories is profound.

While documenting these stories, I began to notice a consistent theme or by-product; thus, the phrase Business Illusions became the subtitle of the book.

PROACTIVITY

Victory more often than not goes to the aggressor.

As entrepreneurs, we want to become proactive in our planning to avoid The Danger Zone and to work towards a successful exit strategy. The proactive approach to a successful exit strategy is the theme of this book; hence the title *Avoiding the Danger Zone, Business Illusions.*

CHAPTER 1

Your Exit

Have you considered what it will be like the day after you exit your company?

The editors of *Strategies Magazine* asked me to write an article on the subject of exit strategies for business owners. The published article in its entirety is included in Chapter 16 of this book and merits reading. The following excerpts are pertinent to this chapter:

> Benjamin Franklin is credited with the adage, "In this world nothing is certain but death and taxes."

That statement is as true today as it was when he wrote it more than 200 years ago. We can add another truism for today's business owners: You will exit your company one day in the future.

Your exit from your company may be planned or unplanned. The exit may bring satisfaction or dissatisfaction to you and your family. It may be to the benefit or detriment of your employees or associates. It may bring great financial reward, or it may bring financial devastation.

The exit may bring fame or shame to your family and friends. It may be the continuance or discontinuance of the company you have worked so hard to build and create. The exit may be to the benefit or detriment of your competitors. Regardless of the consequences, you will some day exit your company in one form or another. [2]

And so it will be with you. Regardless of your intentions or desires, the day will come when you are no longer the owner of your business.

YOU CAN TAKE MY COMPANY AND…

Some of you may want to leave your company right now.

I can almost hear some of you say, "Jerry, you can take my company and shove it." I have heard that sentiment more than once during my career. My wife, Christine, has heard me say that about my own company dozens of times over the past two decades.

I believe all of us as business owners have experienced the highs and the lows of owning a company and have vacillated from desires of trashing the entire company to keeping it and selling it for millions of dollars.

It is tempting to quit too early. Too often a business owner will travel 90% of the journey and then sell the business. Yet, there is a strong possibility that the value earned during the last 10% of the journey could be worth more than the first 90%.

What are your desires for exiting your company? Do you want to pass it on to family members? Do you want to sell it to employees or a third party? Do you want to quit and liquidate the assets into cash? Do you want to work at your business until the day you die and not think about what will happen to the company after your death?

EXIT EXPECTATIONS

I often ask business owners, "What amount of money do you want to receive for your company upon your exit?"

Their answers are very interesting and range from the logical to the unreasonable. But most owners have given some thought to the matter and have a certain amount of money they feel their company is worth or what they want upon their exit. Most can give me a relative range and might say something like, "Well, my company is worth at least $20 million dollars."

Getting owners to tell me what they want for their business is the easy part. Having them explain why their companies are worth that amount of money is much more difficult. After all, the owners are emotionally tied to the companies and are not objective about their value. In fact, seldom can owners tell me the true value of their companies they wish to sell.

Some owners undervalue their company. It is almost as if they are so involved in the day-to-day grind of the business that they do not have the time to step back and see what a remarkable job they have done in actually creating and running them.

Others have unrealistic expectations about what they will get for their businesses. They might have a gut feel for what their companies are worth but they tend to gloss over certain flaws in their companies that will bring down their value.

In reality, preparing to sell your business is like preparing to sell your home. Perhaps your home is worth a lot of money, and you want to sell it at a certain price. It's structure and square footage are appealing to prospects, but your real estate professional points out that you could improve your profits significantly by doing some painting, landscaping or repairs. Your choice then becomes whether or not to invest a little more money to improve your house so you can maximize your profits when it is sold.

The same can be said for selling a business. It is worth something today, but what can you do in the future to make it worth even more so you can sell it at a higher price?

THE CHECK

Ultimately, the value of your company is only worth what someone else will pay for it. This is often a cold reality to business owners, but it is indeed reality. If you want a certain amount of money for your business, then you must do what it takes to have someone open their checkbook and write a check for that amount. Unrealistic hoping will not get you the check, but methodical planning and investing might.

A part of your job in getting the check will be to find the people who have the ability to write it. You may need to develop relationships with people who can help you find a buyer.

Victory will go to the aggressor, and the aggressor will get busy developing relationships that will eventually lead to a check – that is, a check for the right amount of money.

GOAL CLARITY

One of my favorite authors is Ron Willingham. Ron has given some advice that will help with your journey to reach your goals regarding your exit strategy. He has stated the following about goal clarity:

> This means having clear, specific, written goals of what you want to happen in your future. They must be goals that you deeply desire and, most important, goals you firmly believe are possible for you to achieve and that you feel you deserve to achieve.[3]

So, what are the "clear, specific, written goals" that you want to achieve when you exit your company? Do you truly desire them and feel you deserve them? Are they possible? Have you written them down? And if you haven't, would you consider taking time to do this over the next few days?

EMOTIONAL INTELLIGENCE

> One thing that often frustrates entrepreneurs is the realization that they are alone in the organization in their concerns regarding the future of the company. This is one of the reasons for the adage, *"It is lonely at the top."* Entrepreneurs need to realize that, with few exceptions; nobody will ever really understand or empathize with that loneliness.[4]

Discouragement sometimes accompanies those who are lonely at the top. This is a natural feeling we experience while we go through the ebbs and flows of business cycles. We often feel we are pulling a weight that exceeds our capacity.

Sometimes we become angry at others or our situation. Anger is not a primary emotion — it is a secondary one. When we feel sad, hurt or betrayed, we often feel anger. The anger will pass, and we will get back to our natural optimistic selves if we keep the long-term picture in perspective.

I find my attitude improves when I read good books. The wisdom of the ages is in print, and it brings much comfort to my soul to learn that I am not alone with many of the emotions I feel on my journey. Ron Willingham addresses the issue of rising to a level to understand our emotions as we pass through the inevitable difficulties of our journey. He defines a term he calls "emotional intelligence."

> *Emotional Intelligence* – this is basically two things:
>
> It's the ability to understand the emotions you're feeling and their impact on your behavior. It helps you identify fear of rejection and its numerous emotional cousins that, if allowed to rule your actions, can kill your success. Emotional intelligence gives you the self-management skills to deal with negative emotions, natural resistance to change, fear of rejection, temporary defeats, and other success killers.
>
> It's having the inner strength to do the necessary activities that you don't want to do, but must do in order to be successful. It's also the will power or emotional endurance to work through all the ups and downs that come your way.[5]

Naturally, you are going to have some ups and downs as you embark on the journey to exit your company. I hope you will learn the techniques of goal clarity and emotional intelligence to help keep you on the right path.

ILLUSIONS

We will discuss the subject of business illusions in this book. Webster defines the word illusion:

The state or fact of being led to accept as true something unreal or imagined; a misleading or inaccurate idea or impression of reality.

Webster then gives the following graph within its definition:

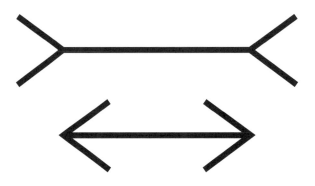

The question indirectly posed by Webster is, "Which line is the longest?" To some it appears that the top line is longer. But this is an illusion because both lines are exactly the same length. The graph, therefore, demonstrates a misleading idea of reality.

And so it will happen to you as your company increases in size in your quest to achieve your exit strategy goals. You will be faced with numerous illusions. There will be days or weeks when you will be working in a fog. You will feel disoriented and confused. Correct facts will appear to be false. False data and information will appear to be correct. Up will seem down, and down will seem up — and there will be many days when you will not know the difference.

You will experience times when trusted people will steal or lie to you, creating an illusion by presenting or representing to you misleading ideas about reality.

There may be times when you feel nobody can be trusted, which is an illusion. There are trustworthy people; you just need to find them. In fact, you will not be able to experience a successful exit strategy without trusted people around you.

TRUTH IS STRANGER THAN FICTION

This book is going to help you identify some of the business illusions you will face as you work toward your exit strategy. My goal is simple — to help your exit become a more successful one.

To that end, this book offers actual examples of business exits. I have documented a variety of these examples in order to give you a broad perspective of what can happen in a business exit. You will see exits by success, failure, murder, suicide and other methods. There is something to learn in each of these true stories.

A few of the stories in this book may make you shake your head in disbelief. But as Mark Twain is credited with saying, "Truth is stranger than fiction, but it is because Fiction is obligated to stick to possibilities; Truth isn't." These stories are valuable and well worth exploring to find information that will help you achieve your exit strategies.

CHAPTER 2

ILLUSIONS

An analogy will help us with this subject of business illusions.

We will compare a business owner with an airplane pilot. The similarity between the two is instructive.

For example, a pilot has two alternatives when the airplane has lifted into the sky: The airplane will either successfully land or it will crash. That is it — there are no other alternatives.

Similarly, a business owner has two alternatives when the business has taken off and is a viable entity: The business will either be a success or a failure. That is it — there are no other alternatives.

PILOT CRASHES

There is much to learn about business illusions from pilot crashes.

We are familiar with some of the famous people who have died in airplane crashes: The legendary Notre Dame football coach Knute Rockne in 1931, actress Carole Lombard in 1942, rock star Buddy Holly in 1959, baseball player Roberto Clemente in 1975, country singer John Denver in 1997, and John F. Kennedy, Jr., just two years later.

> One of the most highly publicized crashes in recent years claimed the lives of John F. Kennedy, Jr., 38, son of the late president John F. Kennedy; John Jr.'s wife, Carolyn Bessette Kennedy, 35; and her older sister, Lauren Bessette, 37. On July 19, 1999, the Piper Saratoga that Kennedy was piloting plunged into the ocean near Martha's Vineyard.[6]

Regardless of one's political views, the saga of the deaths of John F. Kennedy and his son, John F. Kennedy, Jr. is tragic. I remember exactly where I was when I heard about the presidential assassination on November 22, 1963. I recall watching the funeral procession a few days later and will never forget seeing a small boy in what seemed to be a dress saluting the casket as it passed by. That boy was the son of the assassinated president, and it was just three days before his third birthday.

JFK, Jr. became a pilot in his mid 30s. We can learn something from the tragedy of his death.

> Kennedy was a relatively inexperienced pilot, with 310 hours of flight experience, including 55 hours of night flying and 36 hours in the high-performance Piper Saratoga. He had completed about half of an instrument training course, but was not rated for flying in low visibility conditions. The National Transportation Safety Board investigation found no evidence of mechanical malfunction, and determined that the probable cause was "the pilot's failure to maintain control of the airplane during a descent over water at night, which was a result of spatial disorientation. Factors in the accident were haze, and the dark night." The report noted that spatial disorientation as a result of continued VFR flight into adverse weather conditions is a regular cause of fatal airplane accidents.
>
> According to literature found in most FAA-approved flight training books, a pilot's inability to see the horizon leads to spatial disorientation. The inner ear may give the pilot the impression that the plane is turning when it isn't. It takes many hours of instrument training for a pilot to be able to fly in IFR conditions, conditions that most likely existed when Kennedy was flying on his route to Martha's Vineyard. Over the water at night there are few lights, and those lights that existed were most likely obscured by the haze, resulting in the boundary between sky and water on the horizon becoming difficult to determine.[7]

PILOT ILLUSIONS

So we read that JFK, Jr. died because he apparently became disoriented while flying his airplane. His disorientation caused his death, as well as the deaths of his wife and sister-in-law. Tragic.

From reading several books on this topic, it seems that pilots, both experienced and inexperienced, can be fooled into seeing illusions. I find this topic very interesting, especially because of the risk that is involved in flying an airplane. The ultimate risk is death.

Below are some of the ways a pilot can be deceived by illusions.[8]

- The pilot of a light aircraft crashed in Hollywood. He was seen flying the plane in circles and spirals until he crashed, apparently out of control. Tests were completed on the reasons for his apparent erratic behavior and crash. It seems he put a light on the nose of the aircraft. While the aircraft remained out of a cloud, no difficulty was experienced. But once in a cloud, the rotating light induced an intense hypnotic effect that made the pilot feel dizzy. The vertigo was so severe that instrument flying was altogether too difficult.

- The forward acceleration of an aircraft after take-off causes a sensation of nose-up tilt because the pilot cannot distinguish between the direction of gravity and aircraft acceleration.

If the pilot is not fully on instruments, this can cause him to lower the nose, and the acceleration in the resulting dive perpetuates the illusion. The aircraft can enter a shallow dive without turning, and the pilot will still experience a sensation of steady climb.

- Sometimes a pilot's important instruments can easily be misread. The pilot can easily make mistakes over switches and printed figures, particularly if they are not highlighted or are poorly differentiated, and are in similar or confusing rows.

- Pilots can be deceived with what is known as the "Cocquyt" effect. This happens when a pilot tries to maintain visual flight when he has made an overshoot of a landing following a missed approach. He may not know the altitude of his aircraft and may be unable to interpret the position of the lights or landmarks he can see from the cockpit. The nose-up altitude of an aircraft causes a light ahead to appear lower than it actually is. On the descent, with the nose down, the reverse applies to this Cocquyt effect.

- If pilots devote their attention outside the cockpit towards distant airport lights while flying over sparsely lighted, flat terrain in restricted visibility, they can obtain an erroneous impression that the aircraft is flying horizontally when, in reality, the nose altitude of the aircraft is up or down.

- The most dangerous illusions seem to be when a pilot deludes himself that he can see. If a cloud suddenly blocks his vision, he may convince himself that it is only temporary or only thin – and that he may either continue in the cloud or dive his aircraft to shake him free of the stuff.

- Lighting can distort distance on a runway. Bright lights can make a runway appear closer and dim lights more distant, especially when there are no lights in the vicinity. This is known as the "black-hole effect" and gives an illusion of height.

I had a fear of flying in an airplane before I did research and found this information. While I am now more reluctant to get on an airplane, this is how I interpret the above information about pilots' illusions. A pilot can:

- Be hypnotized and fly in circles when he feels he is flying in a normal pattern.

- Become so dizzy with vertigo that it may not be possible to use the instruments in front of him.

- Feel the nose of an airplane is going down when it is really going up.

- Enter a shallow dive and experience a sensation of a steady climb.

- Make mistakes reading instruments and printed figures in the cockpit.

- Feel the airplane is flying horizontally when the nose altitude is really up or down.

- Have clouds delude a pilot into feeling the blocked vision is only temporary when it may be long-term.

- Misjudge the distance of the landing based upon whether the lightson the field are too bright or too dim.

- Have accidents due to faulty instruments or faulty instrument reading.

So we learn that pilots may be fooled into illusions and may not be able to tell up from down, sideways from forward, and long from short on runways and may get confused about reading their instruments.

THE PILOT'S GUT- FEEL

I am not a pilot, but I am a good observer of human nature, and I believe I understand what is going on with many of these airplane crashes.

Here is another observer's take on this problem:

> There are numerous instances of such accidents, when the pilot deludes himself that he can proceed when he quite clearly cannot. Just as perceptual illusions probably have physiological causes, so the belief that it is safe to cut a corner has psychological ones. The American psychologist Woodworth says that the animal 'prefers to follow his nose, look at

the goal and go where he is looking.' The nearer the goal, the stronger the pull. The nearer the airport, the more hypnotic the drive to continue.[9]

And here is my conclusion: Some pilot crashes occur because the will to survive takes over at the moment of crisis and causes the pilot to react to his gut-feel about what should be done at that very moment. Instruments, opinions of co-pilots and other information become irrelevant at the moment of crisis because the basic desire to live causes the pilot to do what his instincts tell him to do, even if his instincts are wrong.

BUSINESS PARALLELS

As painful as it was for me to learn about pilot illusions, there are numerous parallels to business owners and their illusions. Business owners can:

- Believe their companies are going on a defined and straight path when they are really going sideways.

- Feel their companies are climbing up in cash when cash is really taking a nose-dive.

- Experience long periods of time when everything around the owners seem as if they are in a fog with no clear end in sight.

- Make mistakes in reading financial and operational instruments provided by internal staff.

- Misjudge how well or how poorly the company is doing.

- Become dizzy or disoriented with the speed at which the business and business transactions are flying.

- Be hypnotized into feeling too little trust or too much trust in key people.

BUSINESS ILLUSIONS AND YOUR GUT- FEEL

It is going to take the rest of this book to explain the multitude of business illusions you will face as you experience growth in your business. I would like to conclude this chapter, however, with some fundamental principles about your future success.

Your gut-feel has gotten you where you are today. You should always trust it. However, you should start disciplining yourself to verify facts before you make key decisions based solely upon your gut-feel.

As sales, the number of employees, customers, transactions, vendors and other factors increase, you will find it increasingly difficult to keep facts and figures in your head. When your business was smaller, you were able to do a fairly good job of keeping key information in your head – which, in turn, enabled you to react to situations with your gut-feel. But those days are gone when the company becomes so complex that you can no longer keep everything in your head.

When you reach that point, just as the pilot needs his instruments to fly the plane safely, you will need business instruments to make key decisions.

NOTHING TO DO WITH YOUR INTELLIGENCE

What is interesting to me about this issue of gut-feel and business decisions is that business success has nothing to do with raw intelligence. Most business owners are above average in IQ, but few would qualify for Mensa. Membership in this society requires an IQ equal to the top 2% of the population.

Let's imagine that we have a business owner who does qualify to be in Mensa and is a certified genius. Now, let's envision this person trying to run a company.

During hectic periods, he receives bad financial instruments from his accountants and management. Specifically, most of the amounts on the balance sheet are incorrect, such as cash balances, receivables, inventory, accounts payable, debt, etc.

What is our genius going to do with this financial information? Well, he is going to make decisions on hiring people, buying equipment, entering into leases, creating expenditures, investing in capital improvements, purchasing computer hardware, investing in computer software, and so forth. What is the likely outcome of the decisions of our genius business owner? That's easy — his business decisions will likely be wrong. Yet, these wrong decisions will have little to do with his intelligence; rather, they will be a result of making decisions using bad financial instruments.

Of course, good decisions also have little to do with IQ. More often they are the result of a gut-feel that is verified by good business instruments and by input from good business advisors. In fact, with better financial instruments and sound business advice, virtually any business owner can beat the competition. It is simply a matter of cause-and-effect.

THE FUNDAMENTALS

Vince Lombardi, the legendary NFL football coach, is credited with saying

> Excellence is achieved by the mastery of fundamentals.[10]

Those of us who remember the days when the Green Bay Packers were coached by Vince Lombardi realize that the individual players on his championship teams were not the best in the NFL. As a former Dallas Cowboys fan, it was frustrating for me to see Coach Lombardi's team constantly beat my team, which arguably had much more individual talent. Yet, the team with inferior talent consistently beat teams with superior talent.

How did this happen? Simply put, the Packers had a great coach — one who understood the importance of fundamentals. Coach Lombardi was relentless in teaching the fundamentals. For example, the following was reported about this first training camp with the Packers.

> Vince drilled and drilled to polish every facet of the team's performance. He reminded them often

that one play might be the crucial one, and since they could never anticipate which one it would be, players must prepare for every eventuality, must always exert themselves to the fullest. On the first day he ordered two players to run around the field twice, the awful drudgery known as laps. When they ran with disinterested lethargy, he said with a snarl: "If you fellows don't want to give me 100 percent, get on up to the clubhouse and turn in your equipment." Players soon realized they were better off putting out every ounce of energy during the drills than running laps during or after practice. When a receiver dropped an easy pass in the morning, Vince quickly ordered the penalty: "Take a lap." Observed a player, "There wasn't a dropped pass the rest of the morning."[11]

As a business owner, you are responsible for coaching the fundamentals in your business. One of the most important fundamentals is to know that the business instruments your accounting and administrative staff prepare are correct.

It is highly probable that you are being given bad information about your company. So remember, bad decisions based upon bad information can cause a company to crash, just as bad instruments or bad instrument reading can cause a plane to crash.

YOUR RESPONSIBILITY

Getting past the many business illusions you face will require you, the owner, to get correct financial and operational information about your company. While you may delegate details to others, you cannot delegate the responsibility of making sure these business instruments are correct.

The risk of defaulting on this key responsibility is very high. It may cause your business to crash.

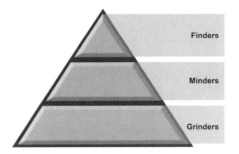

CHAPTER 3

DISTRACTIONS

Gordon Segal is the founder and CEO of Crate and Barrel, which he and his wife founded in 1962. The Retail Marketing Association voted Mr. Segal Retailer of the Year in 1996. Mr. Segal made one of the most profound business statements I have ever read, which was documented in *INC. Magazine*:

> Getting distracted is the biggest problem entrepreneurs face.[12]

The authors of *The Millionaire Next Door* said the same thing in different words:

> Efficiency is one of the most important components of wealth accumulation. Simply: People who become wealthy allocate their time, energy and money in ways consistent with enhancing their net worth.[13]

The above information is critical for your future success and needs to be thoroughly understood. Let's first look at the big picture regarding your needs as we explore this important topic.

INCREMENTALISM

In terms of weight, an ounce is not very heavy. One ounce is roughly the weight of a standard envelope with one page enclosed. Gaining an ounce of weight in a day would not be worrisome for the average adult male or female. But gaining an ounce of weight every day for two years is another story, resulting in a weight gain of 46 pounds for the average adult!

The above illustration also describes what happens to business owners when sales increase. Each day, a few ounces of weight are added to the owner's time until the weight on that time is so heavy that the owner is pulled into doing things that are counterproductive and often destructive to the success of the company. In short, over time, the owner will not be able to do what he or she wants in his or her own business!

WHAT OWNERS WANT

Many business owners are frustrated to find that the people and professionals who surround them do not understand what they, the owners want. It has been my observation that almost all business owners want four things from their business:

- Increased sales

- More cash and personal wealth as a result of the increased sales

- Personal time away from the business

- A successful exit strategy from the business

To achieve any and all of those goals the owner must make optimal use of time. That is why Gordon Segal stated that the biggest problem entrepreneurs have is getting distracted. It is also why the authors of *The Millionaire Next Door* talk about the importance of allocating time and effort wisely in becoming wealthy.

The mastery of your own time will determine whether you will be able to obtain the four goals above. I am going to go into some detail to explain the B2B CFO® way – the cause-and-effect of your time in your own business.

FINDERS, MINDERS & GRINDERS[12]

I go into a lot more detail on this subject in my book *The Danger Zone: Lost in the Growth Transition,* and recommend that you read that book to get more background.

The following graph illustrates how your company is organized today. This organization is present, whether you are consciously or subconsciously aware of it. This organization exists whether or not you want it to exist. It exists regardless of the industry in which you work. Your future success is dependent upon whether or not you are able to properly function within this organization.

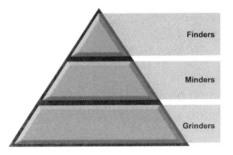

Let me briefly explain the meaning of the above three levels of your business.

Finder   The entrepreneur, the visionary, the leader, the idea generator and the catalyst for future change. Finders work in the future.

Minder   The administrative, accounting and operational staff of the company. Minders are historians and paper pushers. Minders work in the past.

Grinder   The people who do the physical work of the company. Grinders may be construction workers out in the field or telemarketers at a desk. Grinders work for today and are not concerned about the future or the past.

The most important function in this organization is that of the Finder. The company cannot continue without a visionary or a catalyst for future change. The other roles are also needed for a company to survive. The Minders and Grinders, however, can be replaced by others and are not individually indispensable.

THE CANCER NAMED MINDING

Finders open the business relationships and ideas that allow sales to flow into a company. We can tell the value of a Finder by viewing the increase in sales of a company. Increased sales are the result of a Finder's leadership, vision, ideas and future direction.

As sales increase, we see a quiet type of business cancer grow within the business – the cancer of incrementalism. I call this Minding Cancer.

Step-by-step, we see a business owner being dragged from Finding activities into administrative activities, which we call Minding activities. The Finder then changes roles, as is illustrated by the next graph.

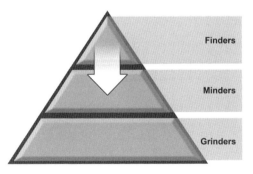

So, incrementally, the Finder starts spending most of his or her time in administrative duties. What do they do in administration? I could write an entire book on this subject. The following should give you an idea about these administrative duties:

- Managing cash

- Meeting with administrative staff

- Hiring, firing and HR issues

- Meeting with bankers

- Reviewing erroneous or meaningless reports

- Meeting with accountants

- Computer problems

- Meeting with attorneys

- Time with past-due bills and disputes

- Government and regulatory issues

I have often asked Finders, "Did you go into business so you could do accounting and administration?" Not surprisingly, they always respond with a resounding, "No!" When I ask them why they do such administrative tasks and duties, I get varied responses – and the responses never address the real issue.

Decreased sales are usually the result of a business owner inflicted with Minding Cancer. A significant decrease in sales will start to cause cash problems. Cash problems will compound and may lead to the death of the company. It is simple cause-and-effect.

Let me put things in perspective: The more time Finders spend in Minding activities, the more power they are giving to the competition. Competitors will be smiling with glee at the Finder's self-imposed plight and will take the first opportunity to kill the Finder's company. They will be like jackals licking their chops over the corpse of the Finder's former company.

THE FINDER'S GUT- FEEL

People are often confused and curious about why Finders allow themselves to get Minding Cancer. They often ask me, "Why in the world would a Finder ever want to spend his or her time doing administrative tasks to the detriment of the company?"

The answer to this question is quite easy to answer. We can go back to Chapter Two of this book, to the example of pilot crashes, to see an almost exact parallel.

> Some pilot crashes occur because the will to survive takes over at the moment of crisis and causes the pilot to react to his gut-feel about what should be done at that very moment. Instruments, opinions of co-pilots and other information become irrelevant at the moment of crisis because the basic desire to live causes the pilot to do what his instincts tell him to do, even if his instincts are wrong.

And so it is with Finders who become infected with Minding Cancer. They typically jump into Minding activities when there are problems with cash, accounting, payroll and other such matters. The Finder used to easily fix these problems when the company was much smaller. The company is much larger now, and there are too many people, transactions, customers, vendors and activities that seem to be moving at the speed of light, almost like a pilot viewing his plane speeding uncontrollably towards the earth. The problems are very hard to fix and often seem impossible to resolve.

The owner then begins to make decisions based upon gut-feel, just like a pilot who is about to crash. The owner often ignores opinions of others and the business instruments given to him (balance sheets, profit & loss statements, etc.) and makes decisions based upon gut instincts. The opinions of others, business instruments and other tools become irrelevant to the owner at the moment of crisis because the basic desire to keep the company alive causes the owner to do what his instincts tell him, even if his instincts are wrong.

All too often, gut instincts are distorted due to the complexities of the moment, and the company crashes. It either goes out of business or files bankruptcy.

PERSONAL TIME AWAY FROM THE BUSINESS

I mentioned above that one of the four things owners want is personal time away from the business. They want a company that can run without them, like a well-oiled machine. They want to be able to travel, spend time with the family and do other fun activities with no concern about the company's success.

A Finder with Minding Cancer can forget about spending personal time away from the business. Things are too complex to get away from the office. In fact, time at the office begins to increase instead of decrease. I have had owners tell me, "I have not had a vacation in three years," or "I missed my daughter's high school graduation because of my business." These Finders often feel trapped and boxed into a corner.

Minding Cancer follows them 24/7/365. Any "vacation" or other time spent away is mixed with minding the business. The owner goes online and looks at cash each day, calls/emails the staff regarding checks to cut, spends significant time answering emails, and so forth. Time at a child's ball game or other event is spent on the cell phone running the business. The Finder's voice is raised, blood pressure goes up and everyone around feels uncomfortable. The children of the Finder, hungry for attention, notice what the Finder is doing and often feel disappointment, anger or rejection as a result.

The damaging effects of Minding Cancer extend beyond the business. Divorce, damaged relationships with children, diminished time with friends, damage to personal health, decreased mental health and diminished spiritual health are some of the results of Minding Cancer.

This disease must be eradicated unless you are willing to live with the consequences of this self-imposed disease.

THE CURE TO MINDING CANCER

There are three steps to curing Minding Cancer.

The Finder must:

1. Recognize the cancer signs.

2. Have a desire to get out of Minding and back to Finding.

3. Hire people that will help the Finder be cured of this cancer.

The result of getting rid of this Minding Cancer looks like the following graph.

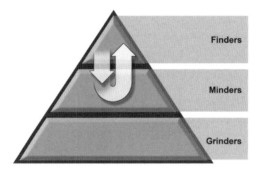

Now the Finder can get back to the role of being the visionary, the leader, the idea generator and the catalyst for future change. Sales should then increase, and the company's organization should begin to be better balanced. This time, the competition narrowly missed an opportunity to move in for the kill. They will continue to hunt the Finder's company. But a wise Finder will create a vision to keep ahead of the competition. A really good Finder will be able to turn the tables and purchase or quash key competitors. Survival goes to the fittest Finder.

Finders should not allow themselves to become distracted. Distraction is an illusion. Rather than simply keeping busy, Finders should be engaged in activities that are truly productive. Ideally, Finders should spend about 80% of their time in Finding activities and delegate the Minding and Grinding to others. Finders should teach the fundamentals as Vince Lombardi did, make sure the fundamentals are being done and then invest the rest of their time in productive areas. The survival of their companies depend upon it.

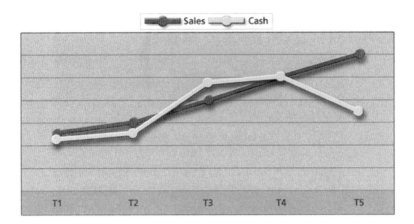

CHAPTER 4

The Illusions of Increased Sales

Do Not Assume The Enemy Will Not Come
– Sun Tzu

Sun Tzu was a successful Chinese general in approximately 500 BC and is credited for writing *The Art of War*. He said:

> Conquerors estimate in their temple before the war begins. They consider everything. The defeated also estimate before the war, but do not consider everything. Estimating completely creates victory. Estimating incompletely causes failures. When we look at it from this point of view, it is obvious who will win the war.

37

> Do not assume the enemy will not come. Prepare
> for his coming. Do not assume the enemy will not
> attack.[15]

Most business owners assume that as sales increase, cash will increase accordingly. This is an illusion. The opposite is usually the case — as sales increase, cash decreases.

Referring to Sun Tzu's comments above, your enemies will become those who attempt to take cash away from you and your company. The competition for your cash will be fierce and extreme. The attacks on your cash will become frequent and constant.

An analogy: Visualize a dam, brimming with water that generates electricity. Liken the dam to your bank accounts and the water behind the dam to the cash that accumulates in those accounts.

A dam, preserving an abundance of water, releases the water in a controlled manner, which not only preserves the proper level of water but also generates electricity (power) through the controlled release process.

Likewise, preserving an abundance of cash, released in a controlled manner, allows the company to operate and helps preserve equity (power) for its owner.

Left unprotected, the elements will attack a dam possibly causing dangerous cracks. These cracks, if left unattended, may cause the dam to break, thus letting the water escape its protection. The generation of electricity (i.e. money) ceases or is diminished. Valuable resources must then be given to fix the dam in an attempt to restore it to its pre-damaged state.

Likewise, left unprotected or without an adequate working capital plan, your cash will escape the safety of your bank accounts. The ability to generate sales (i.e. cash) will diminish or cease. Valuable resources will be given to fix the problems that caused the cash to evaporate in an attempt to restore the company as it was before the damage was done.

Paraphrasing the words of Sun Tzu:

> Business owners estimate in their offices before a sales increase begins. They consider everything related to cash. The defeated competition also estimates before their sales increase, but do not consider everything. Estimating completely creates cash victory. Estimating incompletely causes cash failures. When we look at it from this point of view, it is obvious which company will win the cash war.
>
> Do not assume the enemy of your cash will not come. Prepare for his coming. Do not assume the enemy will not attack your cash.

ESTIMATING NEEDED CASH

I really like Sun Tzu's comments about estimating. This is very wise advice and is much easier to accomplish than you might think.

Most business owners have a good gut-feel on the amount their sales will increase over the next year or two. They are amazingly accurate with these sales assumptions. This accuracy is usually based upon their knowledge of customers, contracts, proposals and other things that give them a safe assumption on their sales projections.

Where the owner stumbles is in estimating the amount of cash that will be needed to function properly with the increased sales. The failure to estimate accurately regarding future cash needs (working capital) can cause a business to GROW OUT OF BUSINESS AND FAIL.

A company in a growth mode cannot survive without adequate working capital. This usually means a line of credit from a bank that will help the company with the ebbs and flows of cash so it can pay its bills, make payroll, etc.

Below are some general rules of thumb to help you with this issue. The actual numbers are not important. What is important are the principles behind the numbers to help you with the estimating process. For illustration purposes, let's assume the following:

Last year's sales	10,000,000
Projected sales increase next year	30%
Trade receivables	1,500,000
Inventory	1,000,000
Current line of credit ceiling	1,000,000

Based upon the above numbers, what is the minimum amount needed for a working capital line of credit from a bank?

We first need to realize that the company is starting at a disadvantage. The current ceiling on the line of credit is $1,000,000, which is inadequate! Bankers are infamous for being conservative on giving adequate lines of credit to business owners. An inadequate line of credit can have the effect of choking a company's cash. Conservatively, the current line of credit should approximate:

	Receivables	Inventory	Total
Current balance	1,500,000	1,000,000	2,500,000
Borrowing percentage	80%	40%	
Borrowing base should be	1,200,000	400,000	1,600,000
Borrowing available			1,000,000
Underfunded existing line of credit			$ (600,000)

We see from the above that the company already has a working capital deficiency of $600,000 on its current line of credit. While this is unacceptable, you would not want to make an appointment with your banker and ask for a $600,000 increase in the line of credit. This would be a mistake. Rather, it is time to follow Sun Tzu's advice and do more estimating on what is really needed.

Looking forward, we can estimate the approximate amount of working capital line of credit needed for this next year, assuming that both receivables and inventory will increase 30% along with the projected increase in sales.

	Receivables	Inventory	Total
Current balance	1,500,000	1,000,000	2,500,000
Projected percent increase	30%	30%	
Projected balances	1,950,000	1,300,000	3,250,000
Borrowing percentage	80%	40%	
Line of credit needed	1,560,000	520,000	2,080,000
Existing line of credit			1,000,000
Line of credit increase needed		$	1,080,000

Thus we see that you should meet with the bank and ask for a line of credit of approximately $2,100,000. A negative response from the bank is unacceptable because without an adequate working capital line of credit, your business could suffer.

Let's assume you follow the above advice and obtain an adequate line of credit. By no means are you out of the woods. Cash will start evaporating unless it is controlled. It is time to do a little more estimating and planning.

WHERE DOES THE CASH GO?

Cash is like water; it constantly flows but not always in the direction you want.

Owners constantly ask me, "Jerry, where has my cash gone?" This is a natural question that is easy to answer — if you know what to look for. Unfortunately, few business owners are trained to read their raw business instruments.

Your cash can follow many avenues of escape. As your sales grow, you run the risk of your cash going to the following:

- Trade receivables

- Employee theft

- Inventory

- Increased payroll expenses and labor burden

- Purchases of equipment

- Increased costs of production or service

- Income taxes

- Increased administrative expenses

- Government compliance expenses

- Debt payments

The following is a brief but important discussion of the first three items on this list; trade receivables, employee theft and inventory.

TRADE RECEIVABLES

I do not want to get into a granular discussion of items such as the average day's collection of receivables and so forth. Rather, I would like to share some insight that might give you an edge by avoiding a potential cash quagmire.

- **Relationship problems** — The failure to collect money from a customer on a timely basis eventually leads to relationship problems with that customer. Customers tend to avoid us if their money is past due. This is the opposite effect of what we want. We have spent a lot of time developing the relationship with the customer, and we do not want money to get between us. The longer money is outstanding past terms, the more likely it is that the relationship will be harmed.

- **Fear of the customer** — Uncollected receivables sometimes turn into fear of the customer. We become afraid of pressing them too hard and possibly hurting their feelings. We tell staff and others to not press the issue; hence, letting the receivables collection problem become worse and verifying to the staff that we are afraid of the customer. This, in turn, plants seeds that cause your staff to walk on egg shells around the customer as well. Customers in this situation often smell blood and sometimes take advantage.

- **We become a banker** — When the customer extends payments past their net terms, we must borrow money from the bank and/or our accounts payable vendors in order to cover our own cash flow. We now are in the banking business, which is not the reason we started the business in the first place. Even worse, we most likely have issued an unsecured loan to the customer with a high risk of not collecting the money.

- **Damaged banking relationships** — Our bank receives our accounts receivable and accounts payable aging reports. They calculate a borrowing base certificate and run other cash-flow analysis from these reports. The failure to collect money from our customers now starts to hurt our relationship with our own bank! The bank is concerned that we may not know how to run our business. They may lower the amount of money available on the borrowing base certificate. They keep this information in their files and have it available to review when our line of credit renews. We then are jeopardizing not only the future renewal of our line of credit but also possible requests to increase the line.

- **Being held hostage** — My advice is to get your business in a position where you can fire any customer who does not pay you on time. Of course, common sense needs to be used for one-time exceptions. As a rule, however, you do not want your business held hostage to the cash-flow problems of a customer. In the long run, it is much better to let that customer go to your competition so they can be a cash-flow drain on your competitors. Get into a position where you can fire any customer at any time for their failure to pay you in a timely manner. Often, they will come back to you because they are used to your superior product and service.

- **Opportunity cost** — The principle of opportunity cost is an economic principle that applies to this subject. In economics, opportunity cost is the cost of something in terms of an opportunity lost or the most valuable alternative lost. Related to the subject of receivables, an opportunity cost means we are taking valuable resources to provide sales to a non-paying customer when we could be spending those valuable resources on a paying customer. The opportunity cost is a missed opportunity to work with a really great customer instead of a marginal or bad customer. The missed opportunity for us then becomes a gained opportunity for the competition. This is now a double insult – we are stuck with the bad customer, which makes us weaker, while our competitors have the better customer, which makes them stronger. At this point, the cost of the non-paying customer is simply not worth the benefit. It is time to fire the customer and move on.

EMPLOYEE THEFT

Employee theft is rampant. It is a spreading disease that seems to have no cure. There is a remedy for smart employers who do some planning to prevent theft, but it is an illusion to assume that theft is not or will not happen in your business.

Whether your business is manufacturing, retail, wholesale, service, hospitality or high tech, it is probably experiencing some degree of employee theft. The list of items employees steal from their employers is endless and includes such items as inventory, money, parts, components, supplies, information and customers. In fact, it is estimated that 95 percent of all businesses experience employee theft and management is seldom aware of the actual extent of losses or even the existence of theft.

Studies by the Department of Commerce, American Management Association and other organizations estimate that employees steal over a billion dollars a week from their unknowing employers. Other studies estimate that nearly one-third of all bankruptcies are caused by employee theft, and it takes approximately $20 in sales to offset every $1 lost to theft. Often management has indications of the problem through declining profits, unexplained inventory shortages, rumors and many other signs. [16]

My book *The Danger Zone: Lost in the Growth Transition* documents employee theft cases that have been uncovered by my firm. Chapter Six is titled "Tempting a Good Person," and explores the concept of how even the most trusted employees, even relatives, can steal from us if the temptation to steal is too great. Here is one example from that book:

About three weeks after being hired by a retail company, I became weary of the controller not giving me the bank reconciliations. I talked to the owner of the company and was able to obtain copies of bank statements from the company's bank. I had a different staff person help me reconcile the bank statements. We discovered that the controller had a three-person scheme to steal from the company. The controller would write a check to one of the company's vendors and hand deliver the check to a friend. His friend would take the check to a bank teller who would cash the check. The three people (the controller, the friend and the bank teller) would then split the cash proceeds. The thieves were caught by the work performed by my firm. Some relatives of the dishonest controller personally borrowed money and paid the owner about $250,000. To my knowledge, the crime was never reported to the authorities.[17]

INVENTORY

Hans Christian Andersen published *The Emperor's New Clothes* in 1837. A condensed version of the story reads as follows:

> Many years ago, there lived an emperor who was quite an average fairy tale ruler, with one exception; he cared much about his clothes. One day he heard from two swindlers named Guido and Luigi Farabutto that they could make the finest suit of clothes from the most beautiful cloth. This cloth, they said, also had the special capability that it was invisible to anyone who was either stupid or not fit for his position.
>
> Being a bit nervous about whether he himself would be able to see the cloth, the emperor first sent two of his trusted men to see it. Of course, neither would

admit that they could not see the cloth and so praised it. All the townspeople had also heard of the cloth and were interested to learn how stupid their neighbors were.

The emperor then allowed himself to be dressed in the clothes for a procession through town, never admitting that he was too unfit and stupid to see what he was wearing. He was afraid that the other people would think that he was stupid.

Of course, all the townspeople wildly praised the magnificent clothes of the emperor, afraid to admit that they could not see them, until a small child said:

"But he has nothing on!"

This was whispered from person to person until everyone in the crowd was shouting that the emperor had nothing on. The emperor heard it and felt that they were correct, but held his head high and finished the procession.[18]

But who was at fault for such an embarrassing situation? Was it the two swindlers? Was it the two trusted men sent by the emperor to test the new clothing? Was it the emperor? Was it all the townspeople that wildly praised the magnificent clothes?

The answer? Everyone except the small child.

This "at fault" issue is applicable to every company that has inventory. With very few exceptions, every company that has inventory has too much of it, so let me explain something about the culprits associated with this business issue. You'll see that, as with the fable of the emperor's new clothes, many people are at fault.

- **Vendors** — The selling agents who work for your vendors have one objective in mind: to get rid of their company's inventory! The vendors may wine and dine you, take you on fishing trips and ball games. They may make you feel like you are the most important person in the world, but you are not. This is simply another illusion. They just want to sell inventory to you. Nothing more, nothing less. They will sometimes approach you with a "deal of a lifetime" to entice you to purchase a lot of inventory at a lower cost. When this occurs, keep in mind that someone in their management has told them that there is too much inventory and they must get rid it. Their job is to shift their inventory problems to your company. Have the courage to tell them "no" unless you are absolutely sure this purchase is in your company's best interests. Be wary of great deals and ask yourself, "Why are they so anxious to sell this inventory to me at such a low cost?"

- **Purchasing Agents** — The people in your company who perform purchasing functions can often be your company's biggest nightmare. Their job, after all, is to spend your money. Left uncontrolled or undisciplined, they will spend your money so fast that you may never be able to recover. Your company's purchasing agents should be monitored and reviewed constantly. They must have fixed limits, and your company needs good software to track their activities. The software should calculate the number of days' supply of each inventory item. Controls should be put in place to prevent the purchasing agent from buying items that exceed the maximum number of days' supply, unless there is strict authority from a supervisor to make the purchase. Also, beware of suppliers that entertain your purchasing agents. Consider making company policies that prohibit personnel from receiving gifts or services from vendors. Your employees can be bribed, enticed or otherwise influenced to purchase goods from a specific vendor that might have a higher cost, lower quality or inferior purchasing terms than other vendors. Regarding inventory counts, you are letting the fox in the hen house if you allow purchasing agents to count inventory. Send them home during an inventory count. Also, consider rotating the people in this position after a year or two. They often become too complacent in their relationships and lose their hunger to buy the best possible product at the best possible price for your company.

- **Accounting Personnel** — Many accounting personnel have no clue regarding the pricing, quality and importance of a company's inventory. They often see inventory as a nuisance instead of an integral part of the success of a company. It may be wise to have the accounting personnel physically work with your inventory for a period of time. Let them get their hands dirty. Have a supervisor explain to them the importance of the inventory, how it is used in the company, why certain parts must have a level of quality, etc. In addition, make sure your accounting personnel do not enter bills into your company's computer system unless proper documentation (receivers, bills of lading, etc.) is attached. Also, have proper internal controls over items returned to vendors so your company receives credit memos. Remember, credit memos are like cash and must be fought over and recorded.

- **Customers** — In 1895, the Italian economist, Vilfredo Pareto, documented the concept of the 80/20 Rule. He noticed that people in his society seemed to divide naturally into what he called the "vital few," the top 20% in terms of money and influence, and the "trivial many," the bottom 80%. "For example, this rule says that 20% of your activities will account for 80% of your results; 20% of your customers will account for 80% of your sales; 20% of your products or services will account for 80% of your profits; 20% of your tasks will account for 80% of the value of what you do; and so on."19 In terms of your customers, try to follow the

80/20 rule. Keep inventory on hand for the customers that account for 80% of your sales. Do not fall into the illusion that your company can keep inventory on hand for 100% of your current or future customers. It is not the end of the world to lose a customer who falls into the 80% that account for only 20% of your sales. Try to be narrow and deep with your inventory, not wide and thin.

- **Owners** — Avoid the temptation to take inventory from the premises without proper documentation for its use. Taking inventory without proper paperwork for its usage tells employees that it is acceptable to steal from the company. They will follow your example and cut corners and take inventory because they see the owner doing the same. Business owners sometimes tell themselves, "It is my company and my inventory, and I can use it as I please." Such a statement is an illusion. Yes, it is your company and yes, the inventory is yours. It is not wise, however, to circumvent internal controls and to give authority by your poor example for your employees to steal. When taking inventory, insist that your staff follow the same procedures as they do when a customer takes inventory. Take the paperwork in your hand, show it to the appropriate personnel and tell them where you are taking the inventory. If the inventory is for personal use, show personnel the paperwork and tell

them that you are paying for the inventory. Set
the example.

Remember, as sales increase, the demand for cash will increase, and the opportunities for cash to disappear will increase exponentially.

Resolve to follow Sun Tzu's advice on estimating everything related to cash. Hire talented people that share your core values. Create good internal controls to preserve cash.

Any failure to estimate everything regarding cash may cause you to become as the emperor in Hans Christian Andersen's fable – but instead of walking around with no clothes, you will be walking around with no cash.

CHAPTER 5

The Illusions of
Chapter 11 Bankruptcy

You have likely heard about the option of Chapter 11 bankruptcy that sometimes allows companies to escape certain debt from creditors. You may be approached by people who want to persuade you to take this option as an exit strategy from debt.

My experience is that Chapter 11 bankruptcy is an ugly business and should be used after all other options are exhausted. There are occasions when this option is the only viable one. This will be explained later in the chapter using an example from a client of mine who successfully used Chapter 11 bankruptcy against an overly aggressive bank.

SOME BACKGROUND ABOUT THE LAW

Chapter 11, Title 11 of the United States Bankruptcy Code allows an organization (not an individual) to reorganize its contractual and debt obligations with the purpose of presenting a plan to the court to allow the company to continue in existence. The debtor in possession of the company submits a plan to repay its creditors under an orderly method.

Chapter 7, on the other hand, is an orderly liquidation of the assets of the company. This title of the code allows individuals to keep some "exempt property" while the remaining assets of the company are sold to repay the company's creditors. Chapter 7 is in existence to sell assets and to not allow for the continuance of the company.

LOW ODDS OF CONFIRMATION

Success with a Chapter 11 filing requires the federal judge who presides over the case to "confirm" the plan submitted by the debtor in possession. The creditors must comply with the wishes of the court and must accept the payment terms approved by the court after confirmation by the judge. Confirmation by the court is essential for success, unless the company has unusually friendly creditors. Of course, a Chapter 11 would not be filed in the first place if a company had friendly creditors.

The executive office of the United States Trustee performed an evaluation of 131,089 Chapter 11 filings between the dates of January 1, 1989 and December 31, 1995. The outcome of the study showed that only 25.84% of the 131,089 cases were confirmed.20 Almost 71% of the cases were either dismissed (rejected) by the court or were converted to Chapter 7 liquidation.

Clearly, the odds of success in a Chapter 11 are very low, with federal courts rarely accepting a plan to repay creditors in an orderly manner.

There are many illusions regarding Chapter 11. I will highlight a few.

ATTORNEY FEES

Some lawyers specialize in bankruptcy laws, rules and regulations. Their fees tend to be higher than those of some attorneys due to this specialization in the law. The court must approve the payment of fees by your company to an attorney. This rule has created a tradition of attorneys asking for a large retainer prior to the filing of a Chapter 11. A closely-held company can expect to write an attorney a check for $40,000 up to $100,000 prior to the filing. Attorneys do not want to risk losing fees on bankruptcy filings, which makes sense to those who have been through many such cases.

The initial check to file the bankruptcy filing is the beginning of a very long and arduous road for a business owner. Attorney fees will likely escalate significantly from the initial retainer and could be in the high six-figure range before the case is dismissed. There is a significant amount of paperwork, court meetings, creditor meetings, notices to secured and unsecured creditors, workout meetings and numerous other transactions that cause the legal fees to escalate.

This is by no means a criticism of lawyers and their fees in this process. On the contrary, the really good attorneys more than earn their fees by reducing debt and helping their clients avoid bankruptcy. You should be aware that the checkbook will be continuously open to paying legal fees during this process.

DEBTOR IN POSSESSION

Typically, the owner of a business that files Chapter 11 is given the title of debtor in possession. This means that the business owner, if given permission by the court, can be the person who continues to run the daily affairs of the business, until the Chapter 11 bankruptcy filing is dismissed.

Being a debtor in possession is often a double-edged sword.

The good news is that the business owner continues running the company. This allows the owner to make decisions, within certain restrictions by the court, with the intent of continuing the business when it exits the bankruptcy filings.

The bad news is that the owner of the company will have a significant amount of his or her time diverted from the business by numerous meetings with attorneys, the court, creditors, accountants, etc. There will also be a significant amount of new paperwork that must be reviewed and signed by the debtor in possession. The business owner will be signing many documents representing true and accurate information to the court. The submission of false or misleading information can have severe consequences to the business owner, not the least of which is possible jail time.

There is a risk the court will not allow a business owner to remain a debtor in possession. The creditors of the company can band together to form a formidable adversary to the business owner. They may aggressively present a plan to the court to have a third-party receiver run the company instead of the business owner — much to the displeasure of the business owner.

THE BIGGEST RATS LEAVE FIRST

You might have heard it said that when a ship is sinking, the biggest and strongest rats find a way off and escape before the smaller rats and mice do.

Similarly, the most skilled employees often start leaving a company shortly before or after the company begins bankruptcy proceedings. They leave because they either do not want to be associated with a company that is in bankruptcy, and/or they are not confident that they will personally benefit from the bankruptcy filing. The other employees, those with fewer skills, will desperately hold onto their jobs with the company because their options for outside employment are more limited.

Thus, the risk of filing a bankruptcy is that the best employees leave and the rest remain. Even worse, recruiting good employees becomes more difficult because of the bankruptcy filing. During bankruptcy, it is often a struggle just to make every payroll, and an owner does not have an opportunity to promise raises or higher salaries until such time as the company has sufficient cash and permission from the court and creditors to keep such promises.

Needless to say, this condition causes a lot of stress and frustration to the debtor in possession. Retaining and recruiting talented employees is one of the most difficult pressures that an owner faces during bankruptcy. Expecting this process to be something other than difficult is an illusion.

NEW BOSSES

One of the biggest surprises to me about Chapter 11 bankruptcy is the power that it gives secured creditors.

A secured creditor in a bankruptcy proceeding is one who has a security interest over some or all of the assets of the debtor. Banks usually have UCC (Uniform Commercial Code) filings against certain assets of the company, typically trade receivables and other assets. Certain vendors may also have a security interest in inventory sold to the company.

Filing a Chapter 11 bankruptcy initiates a set of procedures whereby the courts categorize the payment of cash to creditors in terms of priorities. Secured creditors have priority over unsecured creditors. Often, the secured creditors will be paid in full or nearly in full while the unsecured creditors will be paid pennies on the dollar.

Creditors have power in a Chapter 11 bankruptcy, especially the secured creditors. Secured creditors often have the power to:

- Combine with other creditors to remove you, the business owner, and help appoint an expensive trustee to run the company.

- Give input on the approval of the plan to pay the creditors.

- Disrupt or delay important meetings to be held with the judge.

- Review the financial documents submitted to the court.

- Demand financial records and projections in addition to the documents demanded by the court.

- Approve or disapprove of the professionals you wish to help you get through the bankruptcy.

- Deny or delay payment to the professionals you want to hire.

- Significantly influence the judge on the future of your company.

- Intimidate the company's legal council to capitulate to agreements that may not be in the business owner's best interest.

- Deny funds needed to improve the company's infrastructure with the needed purchases of equipment, computer systems, software and other necessary expenditures.

- Deny increases in payroll needed for new hires, raises, etc.

- Make demands on your time to meet deadlines, attend meetings, provide documentation, etc.

Both the bankruptcy court and the secured creditors become your de facto bosses. They can control significant amounts of your time, impede many decisions you want to make and control much of the cash you need in order to run the business.

In theory, I do not believe the bankruptcy laws were written to create a new set of bosses for the company filing the Chapter 11. I believe some people tried to create laws to help an orderly procession of payments to creditors, with the goal of assisting the company to survive in the long run.

This theory described above is just that — theory. The reality is that creditors often become very aggressive and impose themselves upon the company in such a way that they become a new de facto boss of the owner of the business. This situation is very difficult for those who are used to calling their own shots. This loss of freedom and control can become more than aggravating. These new bosses want their pound of flesh and may use every legal maneuver possible to get their money, even if it means the business owner loses freedom to run the business the way he or she feels is needed to meet customer demands and to beat the competition.

In short, the loss of control, creativity and direction is a serious illusion of a Chapter 11 bankruptcy and should be considered before filing bankruptcy with the courts.

LADY JUSTICE — NOT ALWAYS TO THE RESCUE

We are familiar with the statue of Lady Justice, the goddess of justice and law dating back to ancient Greece and Rome. Well known for her fair-mindedness, she typically holds a sword in one hand and scales in the other. The scales represent the impartiality with which justice is served, and the sword signifies the power that is held by those making the decision.[21]

The courtroom view of a Chapter 11 proceeding is that of a judge at the front of the room with an assistant or two on either side. There is a podium in the middle of the room facing the judge. There are two tables with chairs to the right and left behind the podium. Behind the tables is a small barrier with a gallery of seats for dozens of people who can watch the courtroom proceedings.

One of the tables is occupied by the business owner and his or her attorney. The other is occupied by the attorneys for the secured creditors. The attorneys at the secured creditor table are often very high priced and very experienced at their craft. There are often other secured creditor attorneys sitting in the gallery behind the secured creditor's table, awaiting their turn to speak at the podium. It is not unusual for the business owner to have one attorney and for the secured creditors to have numerous expensive attorneys wearing three-piece suits.

The situation described above is intimidating. It intimidates even the boldest of business owners.

This situation might also influence the judge. At one table, we see a business owner who is either out of cash or is begging to use cash, along with one attorney. The judge sees the collective power of the combined attorneys for the creditors, who are very well crafted at taking aggressive postures against a Chapter 11 bankruptcy debtor in possession. This is where I feel Lady Justice gives an unintended tilt of the scales towards the favor of the creditors. It is human nature for a judge to be influenced in this situation. We hope that Lady Justice will be blind, but that hope is often an illusion.

This situation is most aggravating to a business owner. It is demeaning to have to sit and silently watch as attorneys attack the company. It is human nature for an owner to become frustrated and angry at the seeming injustice of the entire procedure. I have often heard business owners paraphrase the famous words of Shakespeare in Henry VI where he said, "The first thing we do, let's kill all the lawyers."

Obviously, we do not really harbor such thoughts or actions against attorneys, but it is human nature to feel that the high-priced suits are tipping the scales of justice away from the owner, which leads to frustration and other negative emotions.

PUBLIC INFORMATION

Business owners value privacy. We like to guard our private matters, and the circle of people who actually know about these matters is kept very small. We do not keep secrets for the sake of secrecy; rather, we feel it is our right to run our lives as we see fit and to decide with whom we do and do not share information.

Privacy is thrown out the window with a Chapter 11 bankruptcy.

Business owners who file Chapter 11 proceedings often try to keep the filing low profile and hope that the information about the filing will remain a secret. This is an illusion because there is no way to keep it private.

The bankruptcy filing and subsequent documents are public records available to reporters, creditors, bankers, competitors, past employees, current employees and others who take the time to access the public information.

Public disclosure opens up most of the dirty laundry of the company. It tells about all of the debt, how the company got itself into such a mess and how it plans to get out. This public disclosure can be extremely frustrating.

ACCOUNTING RECORDS

The court will require timely and accurate accounting records to be submitted each month. There will be a series of deadlines that must be met in order to allow the system to protect a business against its creditors. The reports must be signed by the owner verifying their accuracy. Failure to submit correct or accurate reports can be devastating to the company's plans for reorganization.

Business owners are usually surprised at the amount of time that must be spent in preparing accounting reports for the court and creditors. It takes a certain skill level to be able to complete the reports accurately. The skill level needed usually means the owner must spend much more in accounting fees than anticipated or desired.

Business owners often feel that the attorneys and accountants have taken over the business and are running and controlling too many matters related to the success of the company. Not only are the fees extraordinarily high, but the time and effort to meet deadlines are very demanding as well.

A SUCCESS STORY

A company that hired me in the 1980s is still in the entertainment business and owns several acres of land with several buildings.

The company's lender was a bank that you would readily recognize today. The bank gave the company a note to secure the property and buildings to support the operations. The loan, a seven figure note, was a performing loan with very few late payments.

My client called me with a distressing phone call one day telling me of a demand letter from the bank. The bank demanded a payment of about $500,000 to cure the default. The default occurred because the bank ordered an appraisal and found that the value of the property was about half a million dollars lower than the amount of the note.

Needless to say, my client was furious. Numerous meetings and serious negotiations occurred subsequent to receiving the default letter. The banker in charge of the matter was very stubborn and refused to give anything on the attempts for a settlement. A foreclosure letter was sent to the owner with a date for the forced liquidation of the property.

A plan was created after the failed bank negotiations. The owner of the company thought the plan was risky but worth the effort. The company hired a bankruptcy attorney and filed a Chapter 11 plan of reorganization a few days before the foreclosure sales date, which stopped the foreclosure proceeding.

We then requested another meeting with the bank. We disclosed our plan, which was to hire the same appraiser that the bank used to do a new appraisal on the property. The bank gave its permission for the plan, and the appraiser was hired. Not surprisingly, the appraisal was approximately the same amount that was given to the bank some months prior.

My client's attorney went to court with the new appraisal. Arguments from both sides were given regarding the value of the property. It was agreed that the value of the property approximated the amount given by the appraiser that was used for both the debtor in possession and the secured creditor. Now we see the interesting part of this saga. The judge made a ruling that the property was valued about $500,000 less than the amount of the secured debt and forgave about half a million dollars on the loan! The bank took almost a $500,000 write-off, and the case was dismissed some time later.

Fortunately, Lady Justice can come to the rescue of those who have an overly aggressive or errant secured creditor.

Keep your eyes open to the illusions of filing a Chapter 11 bankruptcy. Remember the principles discussed in this chapter and re-read them before you make your final decision to make such a filing. I hope this chapter will let you go into a bankruptcy filing with an eye open to the numerous illusions of this legal proceeding.

CHAPTER 6

Nepotism and The Peter Principle

Many owners of closely-held companies employ family members. This is their prerogative as owners of the business. Family members include mothers, fathers, brothers, sisters, in-laws, cousins and others.

Giving jobs to family members is often referred to as nepotism.

Nepotism is defined as showing favoritism towards relatives based upon that relationship rather than on an objective evaluation of ability or suitability. For instance, offering employment to a relative, despite the fact that there are others who are better qualified and willing to perform the job, would be considered a form of nepotism.

Nepotism is an illusion in many ways.

THE PETER PRINCIPLE

The Peter Principle was documented by Dr. Laurence J. Peter in his 1968 book:

> On the personal level, The Peter Principle's practical application allows assessment of the potential of an employee for a promotion based on performance in the current job, i.e. members of a hierarchical

organization eventually are promoted to their highest level of competence, after which further promotion raises them to incompetence. That level is the employee's "level of incompetence" where the employee has no chance of further promotion, thus reaching his or her career's ceiling in an organization.[22]

We see a violation of The Peter Principle as it relates to nepotism in business. Applying this principle to business, family members would be promoted to their level of incompetence and would remain at that level in the company's organization because this principle would give them no chance of further promotion.

The violation of The Peter Principle happens when business owners promote family members above their level of incompetence. It is mystifying to me why business owners do this; however, it occurs frequently, much to the detriment of the company.

WHY NEPOTISM HAPPENS

While I do not totally understand nepotism, I am an observer of human nature and can document some of the reasons why this phenomenon occurs.

- **Trust** — This favoritism sometimes occurs because the business owner feels that the only people who can be trusted are members of his or her family. This is an illusion. It has been my experience that family members steal and cheat a business as much as non-family members. While it is true that blood is thicker than water, a family member can easily justify taking money, assets, and time off from the business and so forth. It is easy for them to create a "victim" mentality and feel the family member at the top of the business is not treating them fairly. One of the hideous consequences of theft from a family member is that it becomes very difficult to prosecute the crime. There is often much pressure from other family members to drop the matter and to not make things worse in the family. It is not unusual for a business owner to feel at odds with other family members about theft and dishonesty involving family.

- **Family Pressure** — The spouse of a family member may put pressure on the business owner to hire that family member and to show favoritism. This is a normal human reaction resulting from a natural tendency to nurture and protect one's child or family member. Business owners often succumb to the family pressure and assume it will cause fewer problems to simply hire the family member and not discuss the matter at home or at other family meetings. Caving in to this internal family pressure is an illusion that often has unintended consequences.

- **A Cure** — The business owner and/or the family sometimes feel that the employment and subsequent nepotism will help cure a family member of some character flaw. Perhaps the character flaw is laziness, substance abuse or the lack of discipline to get a proper education. The character flaw may be the inability to take the demands of a non-family member employer. Typically, the hope of using nepotism to fix character flaws is an illusion that simply will not work in the long run.

- **Learning the Ropes** — Nepotism sometimes happens because the business owner feels that the family member can learn certain business principles only from the family business. The favored family member actually does learn things that he or she can't learn at other places of employment, but the learning is usually the opposite of what the business owner desires. The favored family member learns he or she can cut corners without serious consequences, use unjust power as a family member over the employees of the company, steal without serious consequences, be promoted without earning the promotion, take time off when not earned or deserved, make decisions that are not within the normal job description, and so forth.

- **Exit strategy** — Some owners use nepotism so they can create an exit strategy to pass the company on to a family member when it is time to retire. This is an illusion that does not usually work. Typically, such a sale of the business is created with a carry-back loan or some calculation of earnings of the company over a period of time. The problem with this logic is that the owner has sold the company to a family member who has already exceeded his or her level of incompetence many times over. Now, the business owner is off doing some fun things with the intent of a permanent retirement while, at the same time, relying on incompetent family members to run the business properly so the future earnings of the company can pay the retired owner the money negotiated. It is not uncommon for "retired" owners to be required to get back into the business to make up for the mistakes of the favored family members.

OTHER CONSEQUENCES

Nepotism often invokes the law of unintended consequences to a business owner, such as:

- **Lack of trust** — Telling employees that only a favored family member can be trusted is indirectly telling them that everyone else cannot be trusted. This is an illusion. Non-family members can often be trusted as much if not more than favored family. This indirect message of distrust is discouraging to employees. They often feel dispirited because they feel they will never gain trust from the owner, thus creating a situation where they might not be able to be promoted in the future. Additionally, allowing a family member to steal without consequences gives an indirect green light for employees to steal.

- **Cut back on efforts** — Employees sometimes cut back on giving 110% of their effort to the company when they see a favored family member receiving too much compensation or favoritism. It is human nature to feel it is not worth the effort to give to the employer when the employer allows laziness to be rewarded. Hence, we often see the employees of the company begin to cut corners, work less time, work without as much enthusiasm, etc.

- **Leave the company** — During my career, I have heard dozens of very good employees tell me that nepotism is the main reason they left their employers. They understand they will be passed up on promotions, raises, bonuses, etc. because of a favored family member. They do not feel this situation is fair, and the best of these employees will leave a company in order to find an employer that does not succumb to the disease of nepotism. Thus, the business owners are twice penalized – they keep the incompetent family members and drive away the really good employees. Often, the good employees go to a competitor, which really rubs salt in the wound.

SOME ADVICE

I'd like to give you some objective advice regarding the subject of nepotism.

- **Outside employment** — It is acceptable to have a family member work at a place of business during the summer at a low-wage position as long as the family member is treated like the other employees. When it comes to management or higher wage skills, require family members to go to work for someone else. Let them earn their way back to your company. Let them see how other businesses operate. Hopefully, if allowed to come back to your company, they will learn some skills that will improve your company and make it better than it was without them. Also, let them see that it is a cruel world out there and that other employers give no thought to their lineage. Let them learn humility and how to make their own way before going to work for you in management.

- **Earn respect** — Respect is earned, not granted. You may hire a favored family member and demand that your employees respect that person. Your employees will laugh behind your back and the back of your favored family member, unless that family member can earn the respect of the company's employees. Yes, it is a little unfair that the family member may be held to a higher standard. They need to understand, however, that they must put forth the effort, become humble and earn the respect of others. The failure to earn respect undermines your company and destroys company morale.

- **The Peter Principle** — If you feel compelled to hire a family members, do not promote them above their level of incompetence. Let the family member compete with others for the position and let the best person earn the promotion, regardless of the type of blood that flows through their veins. This will allow you to better keep and attract new talent into your company. This will also teach the family member, as well as other family members, that they must work hard and serve the company to the best of their abilities in order to receive a promotion or raise.

- **No** — I once saw a sign by the door of a business owner that said, "What part of 'no' do you not understand?" While this may be difficult to do with family members, it must be done. Learn to say "no" to family that pressures you to do other than that which is in the best interest of the company.

- **The exit** — Prepare for the eventual sale of your business as if you will make the sale to a non-family member entity. Build the company to that end with that expectation. Then, when the time to sell arrives, allow family members to match the offer of the third party. Show no favoritism. Require family members to pay the same amount of money with the same terms that you would give to a third party.

CHAPTER 7

Suicide

Jacob was one of the most charming men I have ever met. He had bright blue eyes, a winning smile and a fun personality. His passion was deep sea-fishing. He loved to talk about the big fish he caught, and the photos of his catches were very impressive. He was a general contractor by trade and had been in business for about 25 years. His specialty was in constructing tenant improvements for commercial properties.

Jacob hired me a few years ago to help him with his bank financing and exit strategy. His goal was to get his company to the point where he could get bonding financing. He then wanted to sell his company to his key person, George.

George is a very intelligent man and a graduate from Arizona State University. He has an engaging personality and is respected by his peers and the company employees.

George was in agreement of the succession plan and participated in most of the meetings I had with Jacob on the matter. We talked for many hours over a long period of time about the plan, which was to have George purchase the company from Jacob at a price sufficient to allow him to retire and go fishing whenever and wherever he wanted. What I did not know at the time of these discussions was there was already a signed purchase agreement between

Jacob and George on the sale of the company. This agreement would surface unexpectedly about a year after Jacob's death.

To say the company's accounting records were a mess is an understatement. Their software package was not being used properly. The bank accounts had not been reconciled properly for months. The work-in-progress (WIP) system was not correct. While the software package allowed for the creation of a balance sheet and profit and loss statement, this function of the software was not implemented correctly.

The company's controller created the financial statements on her personal laptop, which she took home when she left the company office. She did not use the company's computer system to create the financial statements, nor did she share the information with the assistant controller. The controller was doing the erroneous bank statements and was somewhat secretive about cash. Eventually, she was terminated.

The company promoted the assistant controller to the position of controller. She needed a lot of help and training, but she proved to be a very good person for the position. She was not only very loyal to Jacob and George but was very easy to train. She also had a strong desire to do what was right for the company and did all in her power to do her job properly.

With corrected financial information, Jacob and George were then able to make key decisions to help the company grow. For example, the company had a fairly large warranty repair group that was paid on W-2 salary. The corrected financial statements showed them that this full-time group was not cost-effective. A decision was made to terminate employment of this group and hire warranty repair people on an as-needed basis.

One of the biggest financial improvements was in the area of gross profit margin. Before hiring me, the company felt it was pricing its jobs properly. That is, the people doing the pricing felt the bids on the jobs were high enough for the company to make a good profit. Corrected financial information and discussions proved that the pricing was too low. There was some reluctance at first on Jacob's part to change pricing because he did not want to hurt customer relationships. George and I were able to convince him that increased pricing could be accomplished without losing customers. Of course, we had discussions that increased pricing was necessary in order to achieve Jacob's goal of an exit strategy with George.

George headed up the process of analyzing every phase of the bidding process for their jobs, which was very complicated due to the nature of their industry. He was able to determine the specific areas where pricing should remain the same and areas where pricing should be increased. The company increased its gross margins significantly. Instead of a decrease in sales, they began to experience increased sales. Of course, they had to put a lot of effort into explaining why their newer bids were higher than those in the past, but they pulled it off. Both Jacob and George had a lot of customer loyalty, and the customers were willing to pay for that loyalty rather than go to an inferior competitor who might have a slightly lower price.

The new financial information also allowed the company to analyze its administrative costs and make decisions to make sure those costs were within a manageable range.

The company stopped losing money and began making it. The future seemed very bright for the company. George and the rest of us did not see the dark undercurrent that was happening in Jacob's personal life that would cause tragedy.

One of the first things Jacob told me when I was hired was that he had recently gone through a divorce. The divorce was not a friendly one and took much of his cash. It was obvious in our discussions that the divorce also had a serious emotional impact on him. I did not say anything about his pain during our discussions, but I felt badly for him and the consequences of the divorce.

Jacob was a very active person and suffered an injury to his knee about a year or so after I was hired. He had surgery on the knee to repair the damage and was away from the office for quite some time. He went through months of rehabilitation and was in obvious pain when he returned to the office. I am sure he missed his fishing expeditions that used to give him so much joy and satisfaction.

Jacob's doctors gave him a prescription to help with the pain he was suffering due to the surgery. Unfortunately, he developed a dependency to this drug.

He went into a drug rehabilitation program to get over his addiction to the prescription pain medication. Apparently, the rehabilitation program did not cure him of his need for the drug. He continued using the drug and started obtaining the drug through a non-approved prescription method. He was caught by local law enforcement. The authorities, not knowing Jacob personally, apparently felt he was a dealer of the drug and applied some pressure to get information from Jacob on some alleged drug dealings. We are all familiar with television programs that show law enforcement painting a frightening picture for the accused. Apparently, this scenario was created in Jacob's situation, and he was threatened with severe consequences unless he cooperated with law enforcement agencies. In reality, it is more likely that he would have been given a misdemeanor charge instead of the long prison term with which he was threatened.

We will never know all of the reasons that Jacob committed suicide. My guess is that it was a combination of things; the divorce, estrangement from family, being alone during the holiday, the threat of going to prison and being publicly embarrassed to his employees, customers and peers. I assume that suddenly being forced off the pain medication was a contributing factor.

It happened over a Thanksgiving Holiday weekend. Jacob was alone in his home and was likely somewhat frantic contemplating what might occur to him as a result of breaking the law. He had enough clarity of thought to make a hand-written will before he completed his final act. He went to a local hardware supply company, purchased some materials and rigged the exhaust system of his automobile. He got into the car and turned on the ignition in a closed garage.

George became concerned when he returned to the office the day after Thanksgiving vacation, and Jacob was not there. He could not contact Jacob in any of the usual ways. He drove to Jacob's home and rang the door bell. No answer. George had been asked by Jacob numerous times to assist him with his home while he was traveling, so he knew where to find the hidden key. He opened the door and called out for his friend. He searched all the rooms in the home and finally checked the garage. It was there that he found Jacob's body.

It is surreal going to work at a place of business after the CEO has committed suicide. Confusion abounds in every area. A myriad of questions arise, from "What do we tell our customers?" and "What do we tell the bank that has the owner's personal guarantee?" to "Are we going to be able to retain our key employees?"

The most haunting questions are the ones left unexpressed. It is natural to question yourself, and ask "Why didn't I see this coming?" and "What should I have done to stop this suicide?" or, even worse, "Could any of this be my fault?"

Those who commit suicide do not know the trail of damage they leave behind to others. The emotions of the survivors range from supreme sadness to anger, and all emotions in between.

It was the first week of December when the company's attorney asked for a meeting at his office. In attendance were the attorney, George, Jacob's brother and myself. Jacob's brother was there to represent the estate. We were all given a copy of Jacob's hand written will and went over the contents. George was overwhelmed with emotion upon being given the will. I tried to turned off my emotions and meticulously read the document while the other three were going over the business matters at hand.

Jacob's will was very much in line with what he had discussed with me so many times over the years. He willed 50% of the business to George and put in the dollar amount that he wanted George to pay for the remainder of the business. Reading that part of the will was as if someone hit me with a strong punch in the gut. I remembered a phone call I had received from Jacob just days earlier. He wanted to know the value of his company. I gave him some general principles based upon factors of EBITDA (Earnings before Interest expense, Taxes, Depreciation and Amortization). Jacob pressed me very hard and said he needed a firm number. I explained that there was really no way to give him such a number. He then told me that he had some paperwork to complete regarding a bank loan and needed a number from me. I finally gave in and told him an amount, with a disclosure that this number was really a rough estimate. He hung up the telephone before I could finish my explanation.

As I was reading the will in the attorney's office, I stared at the number Jacob wanted George to pay for the remaining half of the company. The amount was exactly 50% of the number I had given to Jacob just prior to his suicide. I could not believe what I was seeing in front of me and suddenly envisioned the thought that I was perhaps talking with Jacob when he was writing his will. I tried to hide my shock and stay focused on the discussions in the meeting, but I was distracted and very disturbed about the situation. In hindsight, neither George nor I was aware of what transpired in the meeting with the attorney and Jacob's brother.

The attorney had been the long-time legal council for Jacob and his company. A few weeks later, George was notified that the attorney was also representing Jacob's estate, which was a conflict of interest. He also notified George that the estate was contesting the validity of the will and felt the company was worth much more than the purchase price Jacob indicated in the will. The attorney demanded to see a lot of financial information about the company to give to Jacob's brother.

George was notified that the estate also contested his 50% gift of ownership of the company and was taking the position that he was merely an employee.

George and I were naturally floored by this event. Jacob had made himself very clear about what he wanted to happen to his company, both orally and in writing. George hired a new attorney who told him there was some precedent for the estate's claims. There was a risk that George could lose his 50% ownership in the company and his ability to purchase it.

The company had amassed a substantial amount of cash in the company's bank account. The cash was needed to operate the company and to pay sub contractors. George was afraid the estate would go after the cash, and the company might not be able to continue operations if the cash was drained from the company by Jacob's estate.

Attorneys on both sides began to build up large legal fees. A negotiated firm deadline was set, but the opposing side unilaterally disregarded the deadline. George took this as an act of bad faith, packed up his personal belongings from the office and went home, telling me that he would not return. I immediately called George's attorney and said, "Rick, you've got to do something!" Rick called and talked him into going back to work with the understanding that both sides would attempt to reach a friendly settlement and that he would be able to own 100% of the company's stock. Fortunately, George went back to work.

The legal saga of this situation is long and arduous. I am going to skip the details.

George told me that he was sure he and Jacob signed a buy-sell agreement. He looked in Jacob's old office, which had been cleared out by Jacob's family, and could not find one. He called the company's former legal council and was told there was no such agreement. In what now seems to be a minor miracle, George was clearing out some old files at his home one weekend and found a copy of the buy-sell agreement. He immediately sent it to his attorney and to me. This document seemed to turn the tide on the negotiations and allowed George to successfully buy the remainder of the company at a price just slightly higher than what was written in Jacob's will.

Today, the company has flourished under George' direction. The company still bears Jacob's last name.

WHAT CAN WE LEARN FROM THIS STORY?

- A business owner has an opportunity to turn a business around and make a lot of money if there is an investment in getting the company's financial records in order. Good decisions usually happen when a business owner has good information. Bad decisions always occur when an owner has bad financial information.

- It pays to get rid of incompetent accounting staff that do not use the company's accounting systems properly and/or hide financial information from the owners of the business.

- Prices can be raised with customers if a logical plan is created and if the plan is explained to customers in a manner in which the benefit to them is made clear.

- Talk with someone in the event of a bad situation. Jacob should have talked with George, his attorney and others. He might have been advised that his legal situation was not as serious as was portrayed by law enforcement. (I am not faulting law enforcement in this situation – they were merely doing their job.)

Jacob had a first-time misdemeanor offense and could have been advised how to avoid any serious legal problems. Additionally, George and the rest of us would have let Jacob know that he was loved, respected and would be supported through his ordeal.

- Follow the advice of medical professionals. Jacob could possibly have avoided this entire situation had he completed his drug rehabilitation and followed the advice of trained medical professionals. He might have kicked his prescription drug habit and lived a happy life.

- Be careful of prescription drug dependency after surgery. The chemistry of each of our bodies is different. A prescription drug may cause more dependency with one person than it does with another.

- It is an illusion to assume your estate will carry out your wishes unless those wishes are written in traditional and legal methods. Document your will and get advice from your attorney before the will is completed. Relatives act very funny when it comes to the money of a deceased. Some relatives become greedy and do not care about the wishes for the uses of the money from the deceased family member. Tell your attorney exactly what you want to happen to your company and other assets. Obtain enough legal advice, until you are satisfied that your wishes will be followed subsequent to a premature death.

- Don't ever consider suicide. See someone immediately if you ever have periods where this option is contemplated. Completely ignore this as an option for exiting any problems. Suicide is an illusion of escape. Get intervention started if you are associated with anyone who is discussing suicide as an escape from his or her problems.

- Others really care about you. I regret that I never expressed my respect and admiration to Jacob. His former employees and associates still get misty-eyed when they talk about him. They still care deeply about him, even though he has been gone for quite some time. There are likely dozens of people who care about you and your personal well-being but simply do not express such sentiments.

Happy fishing, Jacob....we miss you.

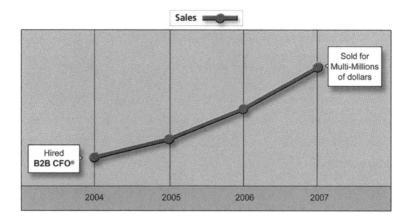

CHAPTER 8

Success

Rudi hired me in 2004. He was bright, competitive, intense and a very hard worker. He was a good family man.

He sold his company in 2007 for a significant amount of money. The purchaser, an East Coast company, is a private equity firm that acquires, invests in and actively operates companies. The purchaser's website states that it seeks acquisition opportunities for companies with operating profits (EBITDA) of approximately $3 to $10 million per year.

Rudi was a very frustrated CEO when he hired me to assist him with his company. His was a situation I have seen numerous times; a Finder who had mostly evolved into becoming a Minder. During our initial conversations, he communicated his frustration at spending so much time doing the administrative tasks of the company. He often had employees and subcontractors totaling more than 1,000 people for short periods of time. Rudi both wrote and signed most company checks.

Business owners often grow their companies to the point where they seem chained to the business offices. They feel powerless to escape the chords that tie them to mundane transactions. They become exasperated at the numerous meetings they need to attend. They sometimes lose hope that they will ever again be able to do what they love and enjoy - the freedom of being an entrepreneur. Instead of feeling free, they often feel they have become slaves to something they created with no vision of how to purchase their freedom.

Albert Einstein is credited for saying that the definition of insanity is doing the same thing over and over again and expecting different results.

Situations such as Rudi's require an operational plan to help remove a business owner from administrative tasks. I try to counsel business owners that they did not evolve into these situations overnight, and it often takes a methodical plan to correct the situation. It is almost like starting to use a muscle that has not been used much in the past. The muscle must start to be used, but in a gradual manner; otherwise, the unused muscle will not be able to respond to the tasks it is asked to perform.

Business owners in this situation are often not aware of the cancer that has crept into their accounting records.

Such was the situation when I was engaged to help Rudi's companies.

He owned about ten different legal entities. The legal entities ranged from C-corps to LLCs. His CPA friend was doing the corporate tax returns and assisting part-time with the in-house accounting of these entities.

The tax return preparation was insufficient in enabling Rudi to obtain business loans. Rudi was not aware of this situation until I pointed out to him that the corporate tax returns were a liability in his quest to obtain bank financing and leasing. The Schedule L (balance sheet) on the tax returns did not tie to the balance sheets of the company records. This was one of the biggest inhibitors to Rudi's ability to get bank financing.

To Rudi's credit, most business owners are not aware of the importance of reconciling the balance sheet of the tax return to the balance sheet of the company's financial statements. Most business owners assume the numbers agree with each other. Yet, it has been my experience that they rarely agree. Business owners usually do not know that one of the first things a bank does is to try to tie the balance sheets on the tax return to the company's financial statements. Significant differences between the two statements may impede a company's ability to obtain loans.

The internal accounting systems had been programmed to report all entities on the cash basis of accounting, which had the effect of not disclosing the trade receivables or accounts payable. We quickly converted the accounting systems to the accrual basis and started working on the accuracy of the records, which were a mess.

Sandra was the equivalent of an accounting manager. She had numerous operation responsibilities and was the person in charge of the accounting for the company. She was one of the hardest working employees I have ever met and was extremely loyal to Rudi.

Rudi's numerous companies created a lot of related-party transactions. That is, the companies sold products and services to one another. They would also borrow money and make loans to one another.

I remember sitting down with Sandra to start the process of reconciling the intercompany accounts. I showed her the accounts receivable trial balance of Company A as compared to the accounts payable trial balance of Company B. Company A showed that it was owed $105,000 from Company B. Company B showed that it owed $5,000 to Company A. I pointed out the $100,000 discrepancy to Sandra and asked her which amount was correct. Not surprisingly she responded, "Neither amount is correct." I then had the training opportunity to explain to Rudi and his employees about why banks and leasing companies were turning down their loan requests. I asked the rhetorical question, "How can a bank have any confidence in the accuracy of your financial statements if you can't record the transactions within your own companies correctly?" A plan was created to make sure all intercompany transactions were properly recorded.

Rudi's companies owned millions of dollars of equipment. Few of the amounts listed on the tax returns agreed with the amounts listed on the general ledger system of the numerous entities. A plan was created to fix this problem.

Rudi's companies also owed millions of dollars in notes and leases. There were between 40 to 50 loans and leases owed by the various companies. Very few, if any, of the amounts listed on the balance sheet agreed with the amounts on the actual notes or leases. We found several loans on the balance sheet that had been paid in full. Several leases were either unrecorded or not recorded properly. Overall, the combined balance sheet showed that his companies owed several hundreds of thousands of dollars more than what was actually owed. Rudi was beginning to see why bankers were skeptical of his internal financial statements.

Rudi gave me the goal of cleaning up his records so he could approach bankers for new money. It took about a year of diligent work before the records could be presented to a bank and expect bank auditors to give a satisfactory report. This was accomplished, and Rudi obtained new bank financing. The new money allowed the company to grow, and eventually a buyer was found to purchase the company.

Rudi, like any business owner, made some good decisions and bad decisions. One of his good decisions was to delegate most of the check writing to Sandra. Letting go of the check writing was very difficult for Rudi to do. I remember a conversation I had with him about this issue. I explained that he needed to let go of some of the Minding activities so he could concentrate on Finding activities. Rudi has that kind of personality where he can sell refrigerators in Alaska. That ability notwithstanding, he could not find new customers unless he was out of the office spending time with current and potential new customers.

A break through moment occurred when I asked Rudi why he would not let go of the check writing, which often caused him to stay in the office until approximately 2:00 a.m. He told me that it was a matter of not having anyone he could trust. I suggested that he allow Sandra to cut checks. He refused. I asked him if Sandra had ever done anything dishonest or anything that would make him feel she was dishonest. He replied, "No." I then put in plain words that the problem had nothing to do with Sandra. We both knew she was an honest and loyal employee who could be trusted. I explained that this issue of trust was his personal problem and that he needed to get over it. I also suggested that he would not be able to grow the company and realize his goals unless he began to trust.

We had discussions about the checks and balances (internal controls) that were available to verify that employees entrusted with valuable assets were doing their jobs properly. Plans were put into place to make the proper infrastructure and procedural changes to help Rudi with his trust issue. To his credit, he let this check-writing function go and instead went out to find more customers, which led to a significant increase in sales.

Rudi made a few mistakes related to the professionals he hired. He gracefully told his CPA friend that he was going to be replaced. Rudi then hired Mark, a tax CPA who had left a 35-person CPA firm to start his own company. Mark had been a partner in the CPA firm and left under unfriendly circumstances. Mark's company was comprised of Mark, an executive assistant, and a staff accountant with whom Mark had worked at the 35-person firm.

My professional career started with a Big-Eight CPA firm. I am used to working around the best and know when I am in the company of a competent tax CPA. I felt uneasy about some of the actions and recommendations from Mark. I expressed to Rudi that I wished he would have associated himself with a larger CPA firm that had enough people to support his needs. Rudi stuck with Mark and paid a price for so doing. Mark developed some personal problems and temporarily disappeared from his family and clients. His unexpected disappearance happened at a key point during some of the initial closing negotiations with the buyer. Mark's two employees left his company, and Rudi was left with a very bad situation.

Another of Rudi's mistakes was not investing in an independent CPA firm to prepare financial statements. I explained that not having reports from an independent CPA firm would hurt his chances of selling his business and that the work would eventually need to be done. I asked him to at least consider having a good CPA firm perform a full-disclosure compilation report. Rudi refused my suggestions which eventually caused problems.

The potential buyer made a proposal in 2006. One of the requirements of the proposal was to have a two-year audit of the company prior to the closing of the deal. The buyer had the authority to select the CPA firm to perform the audit. Rudi agreed to the audit. I was not at all concerned about the accounting records for 2005 and 2006 but privately told Rudi that the auditors were going to go back into old records that were created prior to my starting with the company. I told him this might cause problems and delays. He told me not to be concerned and signed the letter of intent.

Rudi wanted to keep the potential sale of his company confidential to everyone else in the company. From experience, I knew this was not going to work and expressed that to Rudi. He told me that we could keep the sale of the company confidential and that we would tell the staff that he was finally following my advice to have an independent CPA firm audit the records of the company.

Rudi wanted to meet offsite with the key people involved in the sale transaction. We met for several hours at an independent office in Phoenix at 24th and Camelback. In attendance were the president and CFO representing the buyer, the partners with the CPA firm, Rudi, and me. Rudi not only carefully explained the importance of confidentiality but also demanded that all parties sign a confidentiality agreement.

In a subsequent meeting, the audit partner from the CPA firm promised the two-year audit would be completed by November. I expressed my feelings that this was an unrealistic goal. The CPA assured everyone in the group that this was attainable. I simply shook my head and realized there was no reasonable way this stated timetable could be met. Not only was the audit not completed by November, but it took until the following May for the auditors to finally issue their report.

I was saddened to receive a phone call from Sandra telling me that Rudi had thrown the auditor partner out of the building on the first day of the audit. I went to the premises to find out what happened. With incredulity, Rudi informed me that the first thing the audit partner did was to show the audit engagement letter to Sandra, thus revealing the name of the potential buyer of the company. Rudi was rightfully upset that the CPA firm breached the oral and written agreements of confidentially. Naturally, it took some time to get things in order to start the audit. Rudi had the unpleasant task of being forced to tell Sandra prematurely about the sale – before the audit and due-diligence process had even begun.

Regarding Rudi's company, the audit hit rocky territory. The CPA firm was supposed to be auditing 2005 and 2006 but decided it needed documentation on asset purchase and disposals back to 2002. This slowed down the process and delayed the sale of the business by about six months.

Being the consummate Finder, Rudi significantly increased his business during this six-month delay. He should have been compensated by the buyer for this increase in value to the company but was not. The delay likely cost him millions of dollars upon the closing of the sale of his business.

WHAT CAN WE LEARN FROM THIS STORY?

- We live in the greatest country and the greatest times in the history of mankind. It really is possible to start with nothing and become a multimillionaire in this wonderful country.

- Buyers are typically more interested in operating profits than in gross sales. A business owner should concentrate on increasing EBITDA in order to attract a potential buyer.

- Business owners should use other people's money — OPM. Banks are in business to make loans and will do so but only if the tax and accounting records of a company are in proper order. Investment in accounting needs to be made in order to obtain bank financing at favorable terms.

- The professionals we hire should be associated with a company of sufficient size and reputation so that we will not be harmed if a particular person leaves or stops servicing us. The company should be of sufficient size to allow a fallback person(s) to make sure our needs are covered at all times.

- An exit strategy that includes a third-party buyer will most likely require financial statements issued by an independent CPA firm. Planning should be made to have a good firm do this work at a reasonable price.

- Finders should hire the right people who will help get them out of the chains of Minding. Minding activities should be delegated to trusted individuals with the implementation of internal controls to help make sure the trusted employees remains that way. Trust, along with verification, create a good working environment.

- The effort to tie the balance sheet information on the tax return to the company's financial statements will greatly assist the company in its efforts with bankers and lenders. It is key to communicate with the preparer of the tax returns. This important function can be accomplished if the corporate records are reported on the accrual basis of accounting, and the tax return is prepared on the cash basis of accounting.

- It is an illusion to assume a business can keep the sale of a business confidential to all employees during the due-diligence process. This part of the sale of a business is a difficult one and requires much planning to make sure confidences are maintained during the process without too much business interruption during the due-diligence process.

CHAPTER 9

Murder

The last thing I ever expected was that I would someday work for Rick's company.

I never had the opportunity to meet Rick in person. I knew some people who had business dealings with him. They would tell me about his flamboyancy, jewelry, expensive cars, former Mrs. America wife and more. I would later learn from his best friend that Rick had a good heart and was prone to give much time and money to charity and to the downtrodden.

I was used to seeing Rick on the television in his numerous advertisements. He would appear on the screen, proclaim his name, the name of his company and pitch his product. The expensive cars in the ads always caught my attention. He was the CEO of a company that operated in many states and by all appearances seemed to be very successful. He was portrayed in the press as a multimillionaire. He had a large home in Paradise Valley and was a neighbor to professional athletes and other such people. He owned a couple of condos in Las Vegas and drove a Rolls Royce.

The event of Rick's death was sensational. One can spend hours reading about the story of his life and death on search engines. A brief example of the reporting of the tragedy:

He was a son of God…and he must be about His Father's business, the service of a vast, vulgar, and meretricious beauty."
— F. Scott Fitzgerald, *The Great Gatsby*

Like in F. Scott Fitzgerald's seminal novel, everything Rick Chance did was bigger than life. His rise from farmer to millionaire came faster than most; his marketing style was more brash, his marriages more passionate, his divorces more rancorous, again Christian, part genius, part fool. Labels didn't seem to fit Chance and he was constantly shedding one persona for another. [23]

On August 9, 2002, Chance's body was discovered in a Tempe hotel room where he was fatally shot the night before. Several days later, police in Tacoma, Washington apprehended strippers Brandi Lynn Hungerford and Robert Donald Lemke II in connection with Chance's murder. Allegedly, the couple killed Chance while robbing him of a cache of jewelry worth over one million dollars.[24]

Paris called me about two weeks after the murder. Paris was Rick's best friend and was named to be the personal representative (PR) of the estate. As the PR, Paris was the de facto CEO of the company. The state laws in which the will was recorded require the PR to stand in the shoes of the owner and do whatever the owner would have done with the business had he or she remained alive. The PR was asked to run the company for about ten years, until Rick's children were of sufficient age to be able to have some say in the business dealings of the company. The desire set forth in the will was that the company would continue and be able to support Rick's two minor children.

Paris had been referred to me by an attorney who knew I had industry experience and a good reputation. We met and agreed to go forward together to try to help carry out Rick's wishes.

Paris is a very interesting person. A marketing person by trade, he is very intelligent and articulate. He is a man of great faith and is extremely loyal. During this entire saga, I never saw him detour once from his mission to help his murdered friend and take care of Rick's children, whom he referred to as "Rick's babies." He worked tirelessly against insurmountable odds to try to complete the instructions listed in the will.

It is difficult to properly describe going into a business after a CEO has been murdered. Eerie. The employees are naturally distrusting of outsiders. After all, their employer has just been violently murdered. At the time of my hiring, it was not known if there were other accomplices who might have bad intent towards others in the company. Naturally, there was much concern as to whether or not the company would continue in business. Rick was more than just a CEO; he was the advertising personality and face that drove in business. He was a very good Finder. There was uncertainty in the minds of some employees as to how the customers, vendors, bankers and others would react to this dramatic event.

I met with the company's bank a couple of weeks after starting to assist the company. The bank has a well-known name. I met with the principal loan officer who handled the majority of the business and personal loans for Rick and his company. The banker and I started the conversation with the normal chit-chat. I then tried to get an overall feel from the banker as to where the company stood in its relationship with its loans from the bank. The banker is a very nice gentleman and began explaining his position about the status. As he talked, his eyes welled up, and he then began sobbing. I was not sure how to handle the situation. I sat silently, hoping to try to understand what was happening. The banker gained some composure after a few minutes and apologized for showing his emotions. I told him there was nothing to apologize about and gingerly asked for an explanation. His story verified why he had shown so much emotion a few minutes earlier.

This banker had called a meeting with Rick a couple of weeks prior to the murder. The bank was in an uncomfortable position. Not all of the loans given to Rick were secured by assets. Additionally, the financial statements of the company were showing some negative trends. There were concerns about the collection of accounts receivables and other matters. Rick seemed unfazed by the bank's concerns and told the banker to not worry about such matters. This attitude did not sit well with the banker. The banker then told Rick in no uncertain terms that he needed to come up with about $1 million dollars to satisfy the bank notes. Otherwise, the bank would start actions against Rick, personally, and his company. Rick apparently left the meeting in high spirits, told the bank that he would get the money and said goodbye.

Rick was murdered two weeks later reportedly trying to sell about one million dollars worth of jewelry. The banker felt he might be partially responsible for the death. I tried to give some words of comfort, but it was obvious my words were falling on deaf ears. Grief and guilt have to be handled in their own way and on their own timetable in such matters.

The company was riddled with nepotism – one of the worst cases I have seen in my career. The list of family members seemed endless; mother, brothers, sisters, cousins and so forth. There were family members on payroll and health insurance who did not work in the company. It took Paris more than a year to clear out the unproductive nepotism. That action would later haunt him because the vindictive family members sued him and tried to exact revenge against him. Fortunately, Paris had the foresight to have the company purchase D&O insurance (Director's and Officer's insurance), and he was adequately protected against these family members.

The company had no internal financial reporting, other than about a dozen checkbooks. I received a panicked phone call from Paris a few days after I had been engaged by the company. Two family members told him that the company was completely out of cash and could not make payroll. I went to the premises and found a competent staff person to help me research the matter. I notified Paris that the company had several hundreds of thousands of dollars in the bank. He was confused and hurt by the incorrect calculations of cash balances by the family members.

We set about a plan to obtain software and train the internal accounting staff how to keep the records properly. This project took about two months. Shortly after this was accomplished, I had to notify Paris that about 80% of the company's trade receivables were not collectable and needed to be written off the books. This was a stunning revelation to Paris because the amount of bad debt was a very high seven-figure amount. The future viability of the company was now in question.

One of the odd things about finding multiple accounting problems with this company was that Rick had spent a six-figure amount a few months prior to his death in an attempt to take his company public. One would assume the accounting records would be correct in such a situation. I called the CPA firm that was performing an audit of the books of the company. The CPA firm notified me that they were ceasing doing any work due to Rick's death and that the trade receivables could not be audited. They cautioned me about the viability of the collection of the receivables, but I already knew the situation and was not surprised by their comments.

Paris went about the business of liquidating Rick's personal assets. The homes, autos and personal effects were sold, and much of the bank debt was paid. I admired his integrity during all of these transactions and his desire to do the best for Rick's children.

One of the final business hurdles to get over was a very large amount owed to a foreign vendor. The vendor was not very willing to negotiate terms that were satisfactory to the company that would allow the company to survive.

Paris, his attorney and I went to Canada to spend some time with the vendor and its key representatives to attempt to work out a plan. A workout agreement was solidified; however, a subtle side comment from the vendor's attorney to the company's attorney proved to be a key factor in the ultimate undoing of the company.

Paris worked for about two years to try to salvage the company. He knew that Rick had a very large seven-figure life insurance policy that was to go to the company in order to help it survive. In what turned out to be one of the most bizarre events I have ever seen, the life insurance policy was apparently changed prior to Rick's death, and the beneficiary was changed to have the life insurance proceeds go to a family member, rather than to the designated trust. The estate professionals and others who knew Rick's will were shocked to see the money go to the family member. Nobody really seemed to know who had changed the beneficiary name on the life insurance papers, but several felt the name had been changed against Rick's desires. In an even more stunning turn of events, the family member not only hoarded all the money, but I have been told by two first-hand witnesses that this family member would not give any of the money to help with the living expenses of Rick's two minor children. This situation may reverse itself in the future, but at the time of the writing of this book, the two children of the deceased were disallowed any insurance money funds from the family member.

There is a possibility that most, if not all, of the insurance proceeds could have been protected from taxes owed to the Internal Revenue Service had the proceeds been paid to the legal entity as directed by the deceased's will. Instead, the IRS demanded its pound of flesh. I have been told that the IRS settled for about 50% of the life insurance proceeds.

The company was still in operations two years after the murder but was swimming with debt left behind from the deceased. With no possibility of obtaining funds from the life insurance policy and no flexibility from the key vendor, the company filed Chapter 11 bankruptcy in an attempt to reorganize and continue the business.

The bankruptcy attorney made an egregious error and did not tell Paris about a key piece of information prior to the Chapter 11 filing. The contract with the key vendor contained language that gave the vendor a secured interest in the future sales of inventory. This secured interest meant the vendor had a secured position on the company's cash, receivables and other such assets in the event of bankruptcy. The secured creditor made aggressive moves with the judge in the bankruptcy proceeding and ultimately purchased the company for about $100,000.

In the end, an apparently unintended family member, the Internal Revenue Service and bankruptcy attorneys got most of the money. The livelihoods of many people were damaged during the process. Tragedy seemed to be built upon tragedy in this case.

WHAT CAN WE LEARN FROM THIS STORY?

- Evil people exist in this world. Some people are evil enough to take the life of a human being in order to satisfy their lust for money and possessions. We need to be cautious and careful with whom we associate. Heed needs to be taken to make sure we, our associates and our valuables are in safe places.

- We should check to make sure that the named beneficiaries of our life insurance policies are those we want to become beneficiaries in the event of our untimely death.

- Caution should be used in giving vendors a secured interest in anything involved in our business. Security interests given to vendors grant power to them in ways that may be to our detriment in difficult times.

- We should have adequate D&O insurance policies. We live in a very litigious society, and caution needs to be given to this area, even if the cost of the insurance premiums seems steep at the time. It is an illusion to think that an owner or officer of a business can operate in perpetuity without being sued for something.

- Estate planning techniques should be utilized to help minimize income taxes on estate proceeds. Tax avoidance is our legal right as citizens of this great nation. The estate tax field is wide and complex, but good professionals exist who can help with tax minimization.

- Actions that we feel are made in secret are sometimes made public. None of us will escape this life without making errors and perhaps without a peccadillo or two. Regardless, we should consider the consequences to our family and friends should those items become public after we have left this mortality.

- Consider who will run your company in the event of an untimely death. We tend to ignore this uncomfortable subject, but we all came into this life with an expiration date, and those of us who own companies need to make plans accordingly.

- Nepotism can become a cancer to the business of a deceased business owner. As discussed in Chapter Six of this book, a business owner should adhere to certain prudent business principles when hiring family members.

- Banks are sometimes loose with their money when a company is perceived to be doing very well. They sometimes will lend unsecured money without personal guarantees. They will, however, quickly clamp down on a business owner, if they perceive the business is taking a negative turn

- Family members often act in peculiar ways regarding a deceased owner's money or assets. Some family members are not trained or skilled in handling large sums of money in a prudent manner. Additionally, some family members acquire a victim mentality and justify illogical reasons for believing that the money or possessions of the deceased really belong to them. Family members who control the money of the deceased will not always act in the best interest of minor children or other loved ones who are the deceased's intended beneficiaries. In short, greed sometimes distorts judgment and behavioral decisions, often to the detriment of other family members.

CHAPTER 10

8% of the Titanic

This story is about an exit from an exit.

My wife and I spent a week in Manhattan in December, 2005.There is nothing like New York City during the Christmas Holidays. The Rockefeller Center and other such sights are a delight to behold. We were able to take in a Broadway play and by a quirk of fate were able to visit with Shoshanna Bean, the star of Wicked. We spent some solemn time at Ground Zero and were reminded of the event when the lives of almost 3,000 of our fellow citizens were taken.

The terrorists who hit our country on September 11, 2001 caused a lot of economic damage to many businesses, both large and small. Airlines were shut down, which impacted the hotel, tourist and most industries in our nation. The estimates of losses range from the high billions to the trillions of dollars.

David and Marla owned a company that was hurt because of the 9/11 attacks. At the time, their business relied solely upon providing staging equipment to business conventions. They provided the equipment that allows large companies to hold meetings in large hotels with thousands of employees. Their equipment and engineering allowed companies to communicate with their employees during business conferences and conventions. That industry came to a stand still after the terrorist attacks. Their company's sales plummeted, and they were barely able to survive.

A much larger company that rented some of their equipment approached David and Marla about a year after the 9/11 attacks and offered to purchase the assets of their company in exchange for stock. David and Marla owned more than $1 million of high-end staging equipment . The offer from the larger company was to exchange the equipment for 8% of the ownership in the company. They decided to take the deal.

They discussed the transaction with their attorney and asked him to work on the paperwork to close the deal. The attorney had a gut feel that the deal might not be in their best interest. He asked them to visit with me before closing the sale.

They called me, and we had a short visit. They showed me the "deal memo" from the buyer, along with the buyer's balance sheet and financial statements for the year ended December 31, 2001. They explained that this $1 million in equipment that was to be sold was all that they owned, other than their home and a couple of autos. They had cashed in their retirement money to fund the company and had nowhere else to turn for operating cash.

From my review of the financial information provided, it was obvious that they were selling their equipment to a company that would soon go out of business. We then had a short conversation that went something like the following:

Jerry:	"Let's go back a few years (1912) to when the Titanic was being built. Let's imagine that someone offered you 8% of the ownership of the Titanic in exchange for all that you owned. What value would you have received for your money?"
David:	"I would have owned 8% of a ship that sunk to the bottom of the ocean."
Jerry:	"If you do this deal, you will give more than $1 million in equipment to this company in exchange for 8% of the ownership of their stock. I predict they will be out of business within a year or so. You will then own 8% of nothing and will have

lost everything. Investing in this company will give you the same results as would an investment in the Titanic."

David looked at me in disbelief. I was not sure whether he thought I was brilliant or perhaps the most foolish business consultant he had ever met. We talked for a few minutes about what I felt he should do, which was to cancel the deal. He explained that the cancellation would cost him a lot of cash. I wished him luck with his ownership of the Titanic and said goodbye. I expected to never hear from David and Marla again.

Their attorney contacted me some time after this meeting and told me that they had decided to cancel the buy-sell agreement.

David called me a few months later. He told me that he had just received an invitation to attend an auction. The invitation was a bankruptcy sale of the equipment of the company that had tried to get their $1 million of equipment for 8% of their company just a few months earlier. I congratulated them for their wise decision to stay away from the potential buyer of their equipment.

They hired me some time later. We worked together to clean up a mess that had been created in their accounting system by their tax CPA. We worked on a plan to obtain the bank financing they needed to grow. The financing needs were in the form of equipment purchases and working capital lines of credit. At first the banks were reluctant to offer the money they needed. We worked together to do what was necessary to get good bank lending. David and Marla spent the next five years working hard, living frugally but working smart. Their sales have grown almost eight fold.

They have diversified their business in order to not be dependent solely upon the industry that was harmed so badly on 9/11. One of their interesting verticals is providing high-end equipment that is used at the concerts of major rock stars.

For every dark cloud there is a silver lining. The President of the United States signed into law a bill that allowed businesses to take additional accelerated depreciation on the purchase of equipment after the terrorist attacks of 9/11. The intent of the law was to give incentives to business owners to purchase equipment in order to stimulate the economy after the September 11 attacks. David and Marla took advantage of this tax law and started purchasing high-end equipment, which allowed their sales to grow significantly. Sales grew, and taxable income was lowered due to the accelerated depreciation allowed under the short-term tax laws enacted after 9/11. This lowering of income taxes allowed David and Marla to rapidly grow.

Presently, there are several banks competing for their services. They have no problem getting the money they need at very favorable pricing.

Dave and Marla now own more than $10 million in equipment. They recently purchased a 35,000 square foot building and have expanded operations into the East Coast. They are a shining example of business success.

Today, the sales of their company are higher than those of the company that tried to purchase their assets for 8% of the company's stock.

WHAT CAN WE LEARN FROM THIS STORY?

- An exchange of company assets solely for stock options may be an illusion. Cash is king. Beware of companies that make offers to obtain your company's assets for stock or stock options. There may be instances where this economic event is good for you, but cash is often a very good alternative.

- Seek competent advice before the final sales transaction of your company. Listen to your advisors so you can make an objective decision as to what is best for you and your family.

- Take advantage of tax laws and tax planning. Seek out the best tax advisors possible and use the tax laws to your benefit.

- Diversify the lines of business available to your company. Continually look for ways to be less dependent upon one single market in order to prepare for a down turn in the economy or a disaster.

- Be persistent, as were David and Marla.

The 30th U.S. President, Calvin Coolidge, said, *"Nothing in the world can take the place of persistence. Talent will not; nothing is more common than unsuccessful individuals with talent. Genius will not; unrewarded genius is almost a proverb. Education will not; the world is full of educated derelicts. Persistence and determination alone are omnipotent."*[25]

CHAPTER 11

A Bank Exit

Tom and Glen started a machine shop in the 1980s. They hired me in the early 1990s when they were operating the business in a cramped, leased building consisting of three bays and about 11,000 square feet. Their company owned a lot of equipment, most of which was Computer Numerical Control machinery (CNC). The work conditions were so cramped that I had to walk sideways to get through their shop when I did the customary tour of their operations.

The company is not a typical machine shop. The company specializes in the design and manufacturing of very sophisticated metal parts for various industries, including the semiconductor, automotive, aerospace, and medical

119

and electronics industries. Some of their parts go into outer space. This company's ability to create parts that comply within tolerance levels that measure in microscopic degrees is beyond my ability to comprehend. Their operation is truly remarkable. It is fascinating to watch their manufacturing process.

Tom is an avid golfer with a very dry sense of humor. Unfortunately, for those of us who cannot golf, he has a very low golf handicap. He likes to tell people that he works "half days," which to him means working from 6:00 a.m. to 6:00 p.m. Notwithstanding the hard work, he and Glen always seem to find time to hit a golf course. Glen, a dedicated family man, is also a good golfer. He has been running the operational side of the company and is an expert in making sure the company's products meet the demanding required specifications.

Tom and Glen had a vision of buying some land and building a high-tech 40,000 square foot building. They wanted to have a "clean room" to build and test their customers' products. To understand what a clean room is, visualize a room, stark white, in which one must wear uniforms that look like space suits. It is a contained room that does not allow microscopic particles to enter while continuously filtering particles emitted into the environment by workers.

The goal was to increase the production capacity and productivity of the company with the new building to attract new and larger customers. The long-term goal was to pay the mortgage on the building and have an income-producing asset that would have a lot of value to the risk takers.

They found the right property for the price they wanted. There was not only enough land on which to place the building, but there were several acres adjacent that they also purchased to allow for future appreciation earnings.

We put together a business plan and pitched it to a well-known bank. The bank liked the plan and agreed to fund the building as well as the working capital needs of the company. The building plans were created, construction was completed and the company moved into their new high-tech building.

The sales growth plan started working, even beyond the original projections. The new facilities opened up the opportunity to bring in new potential customers. The prospective customers were very impressed with the production and quality control aspects.

The semiconductor market began to open up to the company due in part to the increase in demand for personal computers. New CNC machinery was purchased with loans from the bank in order to keep up with demand. Both sales and profits soared. This was a great time for Tom and Glen, as they were realizing the American Dream and were being rewarded for their intelligence and hard work. The semiconductor business became more than 50% of their overall business, and the future looked very bright for the company.

Unfortunately, the market changed significantly in the semiconductor industry. A few key purchase orders from two large companies were not honored. Tom and Glen had to decide whether or not they were going to sue these companies to force them to honor their purchase orders. It was a David vs. Goliath situation. After a lot of discussion and planning, it was determined that the legal fees that would be incurred in going after a Fortune 500 company were not worth the risk. They were in somewhat of a catch-22 situation because they also did not want to overlook the probable loss of a couple of very large customers. The company had to sit on some very expensive inventory. Sales went down, and cash started getting tighter.

The owners did what they had to do in order to keep the company going. They cut back on expenses and reduced their salaries. They occasionally loaned the company money. Things were tight with the company, but there was the hope and expectation that the market conditions would turn around, and the company would rebound.

The company began picking up new customers; however, some previously profitable manufacturing business began to go overseas.

The bank had loans on the building, equipment and line of credit. All principle and interest payments were paid on time. The notes added up to multimillions of dollars.

They received a demand letter from the bank. The letter stated the company was in violation of some financial loan covenants that were in the loan documents. The current ratio had slipped a little, and another ratio was slightly out of line. The covenants seemed easy to cure, and the owners did not really see any serious problem at the time.

Things went downhill quickly after the bank sent out the demand letter. The bank's credit officer visited the owners and notified them that the entire amount of the notes needed to be paid in full, even the mortgage on the building. The owners were incredulous and at first did not understand that the bank was really serious and was calling a complete default on all loans, even though no payments had been missed or were even late. An offer was made by the owners to put in sufficient money to cure the loan covenant infractions. The offer was bluntly rejected and was not even considered by the bank.

The bank credit officer then began to make things personal. In a stunning move, he told my clients that they were stupid and did not know how to properly run a business. He was not at all interested in the company curing the minor infractions on the financial ratios in the loan covenants. He wanted a complete and rapid liquidation of the assets. He threatened foreclosure and possession of assets.

Tom and I called the bank president. He agreed to meet with us for breakfast. We went over the history of the relationship between the company and the bank, which had been a very long one. We told him about the inexplicable personal attacks on the owners of the company and the unfairness of the position of the bank in forcing a liquidation. The bank president was polite but quite unprofessional in addressing the matter. In so many words, he communicated that he really did not care and was going to support the actions of this rogue credit officer. Tom and I could not believe that the bank president was taking such a drastic position against a company that had never been late on any payments and whose owners had a fairly good personal net worth. We left the meeting with the understanding that the bank had declared war on the company, and the bank was going to do everything it could to collect its money, even if it meant the destruction of the company, which employed more than 60 people.

We spent time trying to determine the logic behind this aggressive move by the bank. We were ultimately told that the bank decided it did not like the manufacturing industry that my client was in. Apparently, the bank decided to get rid of many of its clients that were in this specific industry, and my client was one of the victims.

To make a very long story short, the building and other assets were sold. The sales prices were a little under market due to the pressure imposed by the bank. Ultimately, all bank loans were paid in full and the bank was no longer owed money.

My client moved out of its state-of-the-art building and leased a building. Due to the specialized nature of its business, they spent hundreds of thousands of dollars in tenant improvements on the leased building.

The tenant improvements, moving costs and professional fees were not the only money lost by my client. The commercial building and land market took a dramatic swing up shortly after this forced liquidation. The client lost a good seven-figure amount in the appreciation on the land and building.

Tom and Glen continue to operate the business today, which has returned to profitability. Many of its customers who were fleeing to cheaper overseas competitors have returned and have asked the company to take them back.

Their company has no bank debt. Although, based upon the company's financial statements, any bank would gladly lend them money, they refuse to meet with or talk to any banker. They continue to self-fund their growth in order to not be burned again by a banker. I predict that, due to their current growth rate, they may again consider borrowing money from a bank. If they ever enter into a banking relationship, that bank will be on a very short leash and will never have control over Tom and Glen's future.

WHAT CAN WE LEARN FROM THIS STORY?

- Banks are businesses and may make changes in their short or long term plans as they see shifts in the worldwide economy. Those changes in bank plans may have an impact on your future lending relationships.

- There are financial institutions that are able to adequately take care of all banking needs. It is an illusion to assume that every bank can take care of all business needs. Risk analysis needs to be considered if 100% of bank lending is with one financial institution.

- Diversification of the customer base is important. We never want one single customer to become too much of a percentage of total sales. We want to be in a position to continue our business if a customer decides to leave and go elsewhere.

- Business owners need to know the financial loan covenants that are in their notes payable. Loan covenants in loan documents should be discussed with a financial advisor prior to the signing of the loan documents. Risk analysis of meeting the loan covenants in the future should be considered and discussed prior to signing the loan documents.

- Customers sometimes come back after seeing the grass is not so green in other pastures, even the overseas pastures. The laws of supply and demand tend to swing back and forth for entrepreneurs. While it is true that some products can be made cheaper overseas, there sometimes is an issue of quality, delivery and timing.

- During the good times, bank lending can become habitual. It is often difficult to pass up the money being flaunted by a banker during times of spiraling sales or profits. The additional loans taken, if not carefully analyzed, may haunt a business owner during a downturn in sales, which occurs with most industries.

- An important banking truism not related to this story – it is not uncommon for a business to outgrow a bank. The signs of the outgrowth of a bank are easy to determine if you have a good financial advisor that can read the signals the bank is giving you during the transitional phase.

CHAPTER 12

Shareholder Exits

It is sometimes necessary to create an exit strategy from a partner or co-owner of a business.

Having a business partner is almost like being legally married. There are laws that govern fiduciary duties and other matters between partners. Separating from a partner can often be uglier than a bad divorce. A bad business separation runs the risk of killing a company.

I am biased against 50-50 ownership agreements. Entrepreneurs often approach me about starting such ventures. One does not have enough ownership to make final decisions and is totally dependent upon the other 50% partner to run the business. There is a strong possibility of deadlock in a business if two people in a 50-50 partnership can't agree on key decisions. Sometimes, the failure to act promptly on key decisions kills companies.

Dave called me several years ago from a neighboring state. He told me that I was referred by an attorney and that he had an important matter to discuss. He owned 50% of a plumbing construction company in Arizona. He was an absentee owner who relied totally upon Martin, his 50% partner, to run the business. Dave suspected that Martin was taking too much money from the business and wanted me to look into the matter to see if his assumptions were correct. He told me that he would make arrangements with the company's bookkeeper to allow me to see the records. A time and date were set for my visit.

My initial visit to the company was less than pleasant. JoAnn, the bookkeeper, looked very stressed when I asked basic accounting questions. Martin stayed with JoAnn and me during the entire meeting. He stood over my shoulder and looked at everything I was doing, although I was merely writing notes on their printed balance sheet and income statement. After about an hour of that, my patience was gone. I announced I was going to leave. Martin took my notes from my hands and went into the other room. He came back a few minutes later and told me that he had made a copy of my notes. I asked for the copy but he refused. I decided to take the high road and shook his hand to leave. I will forever remember the look in his eyes as I left. He may as well have said in a loud voice, "I am guilty."

I called Dave and told him that I could not help him under such circumstances. I explained that I needed complete access to the accounting records and the accounting staff without Martin's interference.

After a period of time my request was granted. I revisited with JoAnn at the company's office. She looked even more stressed than the last visit. I closed the office door and asked her what in the world was happening. She started crying and told me that she "could not take it any more." I told her I did not understand what she meant and asked for clarification.

She told me that Martin had indeed been taking money from the company without Dave's knowledge. She felt it might be very difficult to prove how much had been taken.

We began a long process of documenting the fraud with the approval of both Dave and his legal council. The documentation took several months and yielded an amount close to $400,000. Martin was presented with the evidence and refused to recognize the fraud. The case went to court, and Martin testified on the matter.

One of the interesting bits of evidence was $67,000 spent at a bar near the corporate office. In front of a judge, Martin raised his right arm to the square and testified that the money was spent on alcohol at the bar and that very few of the expenses related to the business.

With evidence in hand Dave and Martin held arbitration and settled on Martin's tendering his 50% ownership of the company in exchange for the money he had taken. Dave and his wife then owned all of the company. Martin's theft, legal and professional fees cost Dave more than $500,000.

Another story of exits from shareholders happened to Rudge.

Rudge was in his mid 40s when I went to work for him. He was the CEO of a second-generation construction retail company. He was also a general contractor. He developed land and constructed both commercial and residential buildings.

Rudge remains to this day one of the nicest and best men I have ever met. I saw him work under extreme pressure. He always had a smile on his face and a cheery disposition. I asked him how he could remain so optimistic during some of his most difficult times. He told me that he had not been able to sleep at all the night before due to the dire situation his company faced. He told me that since he knew he would not be able to get any sleep, he spent the entire night reading scriptures. He walked into the office that morning with a cheerful attitude and calm as a summer's morning. I will forever respect this man. He is one of my heroes.

Rudge had given a minority shareholder interest to two people; one was a CFO and the second was an operation person. He had given the stock to these two employees before I met him, so I do not know his motivation for granting the stock. I do know, however, that his exit from these two partners was a financial disaster.

He decided to terminate the employment of Tim, the CFO shareholder. Tim crunched the numbers of the company and presented the buyout amount. Rudge and I discussed the numbers, and we both agreed the asking price from the minority shareholder was much too high. A counter offer was made with the expectation that it would be handled in good faith.

Tim did not handle the counter offer very well. He went to Rudge's church leaders, neighbors, friends and anyone whom he could find to tell them what a rotten person Rudge was for attempting to cheat him out of his "hard-earned" money. I expected Rudge to let this public criticism pass, but pressure was mounting on him, and he caved in to the demands from this minority shareholder. The company was stripped of much of its hard-earned working capital to satisfy the needs of a minority shareholder who was rewarded for efforts not earned.

Subsequently, certain circumstances occurred that caused him to want to create a buy-out for his second partner. He proposed a lucrative buyout plan, much against the outcries from me and others. Rudge had hoped that getting rid of this second minority shareholder would give him the control he needed. He was positive about the future and continued to build his construction retail and land development businesses.

The buyouts of the two minority shareholders depleted too much working capital from the company. His company was not prepared for a dramatic economic event, which was already in process at the time of the minority shareholder buyouts.

Savings and loan institutions, such as Lincoln Savings, Great Western Savings & Loan, and others, began making risky loans on real estate projects in the 1980s. Such SNLs had been deregulated in the early 1980s and some began to take advantage of certain aspects of the deregulation.

Some of the risks taken were to the detriment of investors, borrowers and the government. A brief recap of what occurred to Lincoln Savings reads:

American Continental Corporation, the parent of
Lincoln Savings, went bankrupt in 1989; more than
21,000 mostly elderly investors lost their life savings,
in total about $285 million, largely because they
held securities backed by the parent company rather
than deposits in the federally insured institution, a
distinction apparently lost on many if not most of
them until it was too late. The federal government
covered almost $3 billion of Lincoln's losses when
it seized the institution. Many creditors were made
whole, and the government then attempted to
liquidate the seized assets through its Resolution
Trust Corporation, often at pennies on the dollar
compared to what the property had allegedly been
worth and the valuation at which loans against it
had been made.[26]

Some of the SNLs had been lending money on real estate
and construction projects in an unwise and risky manner.
I vividly recall one of the deals Rudge negotiated. He
purchased several acres of raw land for development. The
S&L gave him a loan for the purchase and development
of the land, which was to be used to construct residential
property. The loan amount was 125% of the cost of the land
plus the estimated costs of improvement. I knew this was
not a wise economic thing for the S&L to do for a customer.
I challenged Rudge and his partner on the matter and was
told that this was standard operating procedure for real
estate transactions with the SNLs and that I should not
worry about such things.

Congress has a habit of enacting laws which affect the
behavioral habits of taxpayers. A series of laws passed

in less than a decade caused a significant decrease in the value of land that was financed by S&Ls.

The Economic Recovery Tax Act of 1981 impacted the growth of commercial real estate. That law allowed owners of certain commercial real estate to accelerate the depreciation of their investments, which caused many people to invest in commercial real estate because of the significant tax advantages. Some invested in these properties regardless of whether or not they were economically viable.

The Tax Reform Act of 1986 took away the tax advantages of the accelerated depreciation allowed by Congress in the law passed in 1981.

A law was passed in 1989 that put a nail in the coffin of many S&Ls:

> The Financial Recovery and Enforcement Act of 1989 required savings and loans to reclassify their assets at market value instead of book value and to sell any investments in junk bonds. That put a huge number of savings and loans instantly in the red and in line for seizure by the RTC. [27] (Resolution Trust Corp, a U.S. Government agency)

Eventually, the loan portfolios of many SNLs were determined to be under secured, and the government took swift and immediate action against these companies by shutting down many of their operations, seizing assets and freezing lending abilities. Land values plummeted accordingly.

Almost all of Rudge's loans were with one of these S&Ls, whose assets were soon foreclosed by the government. The S&L immediately cut off all available funds to Rudge and his company, both in terms of working capital lines of credit and for other projects.

The combination of the lack of working capital due to the minority shareholder buyouts and the real estate crisis created a situation where Rudge could not obtain conventional financing from banks. He ran out of working capital.

Rudge's second-generation business that employed about 65 people soon filed bankruptcy and the doors were closed permanently soon thereafter.

To this day, I feel Rudge would have made it through the S&L crisis had he not paid so much money to these minority shareholders. In retrospect, he should have either paid them significantly less money or should have simply let them sit on their stock until a future date. Regardless, I saw the closing of a second-generation company, the loss of employment for about 65 good people and suffering inflicted upon a very good man.

The reassuring part of this story is that Rudge ended up doing very well in life. I had been told that he is like a cat, always landing on his feet. I am sure a lot of that good fortune is because he is such a good person, a great family man and a person of great faith. After all is said and done, the nice guys often do end up winning.

WHAT CAN WE LEARN FROM THESE STORIES?

- Co-owners of a business need to keep an ever-present eye on the financial records of a company. Failure to watch the use of funds by shareholders may result in one party taking more money than agreed upon.

- Co-owners guilty of taking too much money from the company will not always readily agree to repay the money taken. They have, after all, already shown their lack of character by their theft. They will likely fight very hard to keep their ownership in the company even if they have done harm to another owner.

- Minority shareholders should not be given stock in a company. Business owners often do this to keep key employees in the company. Minority shareholders who are gifted the stock will rarely appreciate the value of the gift. They have not, after all, made the sacrifices or taken the risks associated with gaining the company's stock. Any buyout of a minority shareholder should be done so with the best interest of the company in mind. An objective third-party appraisal should be prepared. Most importantly, terms should be set by the majority shareholder that will ensure the best working capital situation for the payout, even if the payout is over a long period of time.

- The past history or longevity of a business has no impact on its ability to survive in the future.

- Tax laws and other events can cause a company to be severely impacted in terms of its working capital. Adequate working capital must be preserved to be able to weather the storms of such circumstances.

- Lending institutions are not always there for a company. They are subject to regulators, tax laws and normal business cycles. A company sometimes needs to spread its debt amount several lending institutions.

- People get greedy when money is involved. One of the oddities in life is, from my perspective, that the people who truly do not understand the difficulty of earning money are usually the ones who become the greediest.

- The exit of minority shareholders or co-owners can be a very expensive process in terms of both financial and emotional health.

- It is an illusion to assume Congress will not change tax laws in the future. It is prudent to make decisions based upon the economic viability of the transaction regardless of the tax laws in effect at the time of the decision.

- If given the opportunity, a business owner should keep all the stock of the company. Other creative financial arrangements should be made in lieu of granting ownership to a minority shareholder.

CHAPTER 13

Chapter 11 to a Sale

Maya was the CEO of a fourth-generation manufacturing company. She was bright, articulate and a very good Finder. Her company manufactured clothing material for the military of the U.S. Government. She was very proud of the quality of the material her company made as well as the uses of her product. At its peak, her company employed 250 people with a payroll of $4 million.

I was referred to her by the advice of her attorney. Maya called me about a week after she discovered that her "trusted" controller, a ten-year employee, had stolen almost $1 million in cash from the company. I go into some detail about this theft in Chapter 6 of *The Danger Zone, Lost in the Growth Transition*. The embezzlement would eventually lead to the bankruptcy and sale of her company. The event was reported in the Business Journal as follows:

> (Maya) lost her company because a trusted employee embezzled almost $1 million, which financially ruined her business. (The employee) was convicted of the crime and started a three-year jail sentence last April, according to Maricopa County Superior Court records.
>
> Embezzlement is defined legally as the "fraudulent appropriation of property by a person to whom it has been entrusted."

> Louise, one of (the company's) managers who lost her job, describes it as a betrayal by her co-worker that "feels like finding out the neighbor that you thought a lot of is a mass murderer."
>
> Certified public accountants and attorneys report this type of white-collar crime happens often to small businesses because owners are less likely to take the precautions necessary to prevent embezzlement.
>
> Small businesses tend to fall prey to this swindle because they often give too much financial control to one trusted employee, and often don't have the checks and balances in place to prevent it.[28]

The theft of money was used to support an addiction to a prescription drug that was purchased on the black market.

Maya thought she was adequately protected from embezzlement. At one time she had a $1 million theft insurance policy. Cash started getting tight because of the theft. Prior to being caught, her trusted controller approached her with a cost-savings plan, which included reducing the $1 million theft insurance policy to $100,000. Sadly, Maya followed the advice of her controller. Maya later told me that she felt she was thus robbed twice by this formerly trusted employee.

Many closely held companies are reluctant to have an independent CPA firm perform audits, unaudited reviews (UARs) or compilations due to the cost or inconvenience of these services. Maya not only had her CPA firm issue

UARs on her company, but she had them issue these reports quarterly! In a sworn deposition, she later stated in so many words that she completely relied upon her CPA firm with their quarterly UARs to protect her from the embezzlement. She verbally told the partner of the CPA firm that she was concerned about this matter and had the understanding that she was being covered by her CPA firm.

Maya sued her CPA firm for their alleged negligence in the embezzlement.

This issue of embezzlement and the services of a CPA firm is a constant theme that comes up in conversations with business owners and the partners of my firm. My previous writing on this subject merits review:

> Many business owners ask B2B CFO® if their CPA or CPA firm can perform the function of looking over the shoulders of the controller. This is a good and legitimate question.
>
> Certain, but not all, CPA firms can be hired to perform fraud examinations. This is a specific engagement that will last for the limited period of time that the CPA firm is engaged.
>
> CPA firms are usually engaged to perform tax returns, audits, unaudited reviews and/or compilations. *They should not be relied upon for fraud detection when they perform any of these engagements, unless the engagement letter specifically spells out the terms of the fraud detection.*

It is not fair to the business owner or the CPA firm to expect fraud detection unless the scope of work is so defined in the CPAs engagement letter. Read the engagement letter from your CPA very carefully. Most audit, compilation and unaudited review engagement letters will say something like, *"Our engagement cannot be relied upon to disclose errors, illegal acts, fraud or any theft that may exist in your company."*

Again, there is nothing wrong with your CPA making this type of statement; you just need to be aware that the scope of the CPA's work (unless so specified) will most likely not uncover any fraud or theft that may exist in your company.[29]

Telling Maya the above information was of no comfort. She felt as if she had now been thrice betrayed: by her controller, the decreased theft insurance policy and her CPA firm. She was frustrated beyond words.

Significant adjustments to inventory, accounts payable and other items on the balance sheet needed to be made to correct the company's financial statements from the embezzlement. The corrections to the internal financial statements were not to the liking of the company's bank that had issued a line of credit. We had numerous meetings with the bank in an attempt to work out a plan of action. The bank became stubborn and froze the line of credit. Maya had previously thought she had a great relationship with the bank and now felt betrayed for the fourth time. Chapter 11 bankruptcy seemed like the only viable option for reorganization, and a plan was submitted to the courts.

Maya was starting to succeed with the Chapter 11 reorganization. Her customer base continued working with her, which is a great testament to her ethics and abilities. Her vendors continued to provide material to her. The biggest challenge was the lone secured creditor, the bank. The bank became hostile and would not work with her on the plan of reorganization. They put a lot of pressure on the company with constant meetings, demands, delays with the courts and so forth.

I had numerous meetings with Maya during this long period of time. I felt upbeat about her company, but the emotional toll was showing. She felt she was carrying too much weight on her shoulders with the constant dealings of employing 150 people, negotiations with the U.S. Government on purchase orders, buying of material from vendors, paperwork and legal fees for the Chapter 11 filing and the never-ending whining from the bank. She was simply worn down, although I think there was more to the story than just these issues.

I feel Maya was afraid another shoe would unexpectedly drop. She felt betrayed by her employee, the CPA firm, the bank and others. In retrospect, I can see why she felt there might be yet another surprise betrayal in the future. She decided to sell the company.

Several offers were considered, and she settled on a buyer that owned a manufacturing plant in Texas. The offer was submitted, and we kicked it around for a while. I told her the offering price was too low. The CEO of the buying company made a compelling offer telling her that she could not only escape all of her financial worries by the sale of her company but she could also have a lot of freedom and money by becoming the lead sales person for his company. He offered her a potentially lucrative employment agreement.

Maya and I flew to Texas to meet with the buyer's key people prior to the signing of the buy-sell agreement. The CEO picked us up in a black Mercedes at the airport. The CEO was a tall man. Maya and I would soon learn that he was also vulgar. I was shocked to see him make a sexual advance to my client within the first two hours of our meeting. I was incredulous that anyone would make such a sexual advance, much less one CEO to another in front of a financial advisor.

The buyer's operation was very impressive. He had around 700 employees who manufactured clothing apparel. The manufacturing plant was run with extreme efficiency. Maya felt comfortable selling her equipment and intellectual property to this company. She had great expectations of relief from the pressure of a CEO. The sale was made. The equipment was transferred from Arizona to Texas. About 150 Arizona employees lost their jobs.

Regarding the loss of jobs of Maya's employees, the Business Journal wrote, "'I feel like I let them down," (Maya) said of her workers, most of whom are women and minorities. "They all have kids. What are they going to do?"[30]

I had the pleasure of visiting with Maya about a year or so after the sale of her business. She was looking great, full of life and energy. She notified me that she was no longer employed by the buyer of her company and had successfully sued the CEO for sexual harassment.

WHAT CAN WE LEARN FROM THIS STORY?

- Employee theft occurs. Internal controls need to be in place to guard against theft.

- Someone other than your CPA firm needs to watch over the shoulders of your controller and accounting staff. While nobody can guarantee that theft will not occur in your business, common sense dictates that a monthly visit by a qualified outside party might help deter theft.

- CPA firms can't be relied upon to uncover theft unless there is a specific engagement letter that specifies the scope and time period for the fraud audit.

- Most banks will become unfriendly to a business once the numbers begin to slip regardless of the longevity of the business relationship.

- Chapter 11 is sometimes a vehicle to be used to give a company time to reorganize and sell its assets and/or intellectual property for a fair-market value.

- Sexual harassment at any level is against the law. Anyone involved in committing such an act should be prepared for litigation.

- It is an illusion to operate a business without theft and fraud insurance. A review of the scope and terms of the coverage should be made by the CEO on an annual basis. This is a decision that should not be delegated by the CEO. Advice and consultation should be considered from competent insurance, legal and other advisors.

CHAPTER 14

Chapter 11 to Chapter 7

Ronald was an owner of a retail business that sold appliances and televisions. About 75% of the sales of his company related to white-good appliances – refrigerators, freezers, washers, dryers and so forth.

He had been in business for quite some time before he hired me. He was a 40% minority shareholder at the time. We worked on a plan that eventually gave him 100% of the stock ownership of the company.

Ronald was a good family man and was fun to work with. He was a good Finder and was very attentive to each and every customer that entered his retail stores. He spent a lot of money advertising in newspapers and television. We were able to improve his advertising with an aggressive move to increase money from the makers of his products.

Given that retail is a very tough business, we worked for years to improve it. He made a good living and employed about 55 people. At the height of the business, the sales exceeded $25 million. Ronald began building a good retirement fund.

Cash is king, and we created a plan to save cash. It took many after-tax years of work to build up a comfortable amount of cash in the bank. The owner of the building that

Ronald's company leased approached him one day and told him they were not going to allow him to extend the lease of the building in which he had been operating for many years.

Ronald began looking for a new building to lease. The real estate agent he hired showed him some land and suggested the possibility of purchasing the land for the purpose of constructing a retail store. Ronald liked the idea and signed an agreement to purchase the land. I explained to him that while I understood his desire to own his building, the down payment required to obtain the building loan would take most of the hard-earned after-tax cash that he had saved. Ever the optimist, Ronald decided to take the risk and started construction of the building.

Around the time of this decision, several big-box stores started entering the market, most notably, Lowe's and Home Depot. These companies were well known for selling home improvement products. They both decided to start selling white-good appliances, which really disturbed Ronald. He constantly visited these stores and write down the various sales prices. He met with those of us in his management team and complained about the low prices of the products sold in these stores.

Ronald decided to hire David, an expert in the appliance industry. David knew most of the key players at the companies that manufactured white-good appliances and had a wealth of knowledge and experience.

David proposed a simple plan to Ronald that, if followed, might have been able to save his business. David suggested the company change its strategy in inventory from wide and narrow to narrow and deep.

David taught that with these types of products, retail consumers needed options when contemplating a purchase. They needed the product presented with three price choices – low, medium and high. Since many of the purchase decisions were often impulsive, David suggested that the company stock a lot of inventory with these three choices so the customer could purchase the merchandise on the spot. The merchandise could either then be taken by the customer or immediately delivered.

Ronald did not like this idea. He was used to the "old" way of managing inventory. He liked carrying inventory in the wide and narrow method. That meant he liked to carry a lot of inventory so customers would have a wide selection from which to choose. This method meant his company had to carry a seven-figure inventory amount that was very slow in inventory turns.

The big-box stores began to become very competitive with each other in terms of pricing. They were experts in the narrow and deep method of inventory. They gave very few choices to the consumer but had plenty of products on hand with very favorable financing terms. David had some industry experience and explained these big-box stores were purchasing and selling so much inventory that the manufacturers began to significantly lower their wholesale price. This economic event allowed the big-boxes to lower their prices even more, which drastically ate into Ronald's sales and profits. Cash dried up, and he was left with a lot of inventory at prices that were not appealing to the consumer.

I was stunned to learn that Ronald depleted his retirement savings in order to keep the business going, which had been built up over a long period of time. After learning about this, I asked him to put the money back into his retirement funds. I told him that he needed that money should the company fail to continue. He told me not to worry about things.

Ronald and I met with his local competitor at Ronald's house in a lengthy meeting to talk about selling the business. The negotiations were successful, and a buy-sell agreement was created that would have given Ronald enough money to get out of his situation and to live comfortably. We both made a preliminary review of the final buy-sell agreement. We then set a time to go to the competitor's office to sign the final paperwork and to begin the transition of merging the two companies. Ronald picked up the pen and, prior to signing the document, told the buyer that he should have his health insurance paid for the next several years. I tried to signal to Ronald that this was not a good move to make at this stage of the sale. He winked at me and continued to press the buyer. The chairman of the company apparently was not in a good mood. He exploded and told us the deal was off – permanently.

Ronald went back to work, but the company was soon out of cash. He made the decision to not pay state sales taxes because he lacked operating cash. The bill soon accumulated to around $250,000. I pleaded with him to go with me to the state sales tax division to work out a plan to pay the bill. He told me that he had been in this situation many times before during his 35 years of running the business, and those things would work out.

Things did not work out. The state imposed a lien on the company's cash accounts. The company was then in a position of not making its payroll. Ronald consulted with an attorney and filed Chapter 11.

The companies that lent money on the inventory (flooring lines) were not pleased with the Chapter 11 filing, especially upon learning that the state sales taxes had not been paid. This situation caused the Chapter 11 judge to place the state in a superior position to the secured creditors. In a short period of time, the company filed Chapter 7 bankruptcy. The inventory was liquidated, and the company closed its doors after about 35 years of business.

WHAT CAN WE LEARN FROM THIS STORY?

- Pay federal and state taxes on a timely basis. The government has the power to place liens on cash accounts and is often not reluctant to act quickly against a company. The government is often impartial to issues of a company's ability to make payroll, etc.

- The government may work with a company that is behind on paying its taxes, but it is an illusion to assume they will always do so or that the work-out plan will always be one that is satisfactory.

- Do not use working capital to fund the construction of a building. The down payment should come from sources other than working capital.

- Don't haggle over small items when negotiating the sale of a business. It is not wise to propose changes to a deal after it is written and ready to sign unless one is willing to take the risk of the sale not going through.

- Be flexible and bend with the competition. Know the trends of the customer and be willing to do what is necessary to beat the competition at their own game.

- Keep inventory lean. It is better to risk losing a few customers than to carry too much inventory on hand, which will not only use working capital, but might eventually lead to losing more than a few customers.

- Leave retirement savings alone. That money should be set aside for retirement and should not be used to fund a sinking ship.

- Secured creditors can't be counted as friends in a Chapter 11 environment. They will take any action needed to protect their secured position, even if the action leads to the eventual closing of a long-term business.

Cecil L. Mills, far right, 1937, Oklahoma coal mine

CHAPTER 15

A Rising Tide
Raises All Ships

Qualified labor will become one of the greatest hurdles to the growth of many companies over the next few decades. Business owners will find access to money, equipment, buildings, computers, software and technology. Their biggest business challenge may be the acquisition of enough qualified labor. This may make growth difficult for many companies. It may have a negative impact on the successful exit strategies for many entrepreneurs.

One of the reasons for the challenges for qualified labor is demographic. The baby-boom generation, those 75 million or so born between 1946 to 1964, are retired or in the process of retiring. The subsequent populations, Generations X, Y, Z and beyond, are not only fewer in number but also have a different work ethic than past generations.

PAST-GENERATION WORK ETHICS

As a child, I spent time with my grandfather, Cecil L. Mills. He was a former coal miner who was drafted in the Navy during World War II and spent time on a Kaiser ship. He served four years in the military and participated in the invasion of the Philippines., He once went without sleep for five days as a radar operator. He also served in Okinawa. He told me, "My family was sent $180 a month while I was in the Service. I wouldn't take a million dollars for that experience and I wouldn't give you a dime for another just like it."

My grandmother, Opal, raised six small children while my grandfather served our country in WWII. My grandmother is one of the few people I have met in life who will have a free pass to get through the proverbial Pearly Gates. She was an angel. My fondest childhood memories are of time spent in her kitchen. The wonderful smell of freshly-baked pies, her gentle smile and her constant singing of uplifting songs were heaven to me. Her father, George Washington Mullen, was born in 1885 in Missouri. His father, Michael was born in 1838 in New York City. My grandmother believed he was born on Ellis Island. His parents, Mike and Elisabeth Mae, immigrated from Ireland.

After WWII, my grandparents moved from the coal mines of Oklahoma to the State of Washington. They purchased an apple orchard and became entrepreneurs. They successfully raised eight children.

My grandfather was the most intimidating man I have ever met. I listened carefully to every word he said and followed his instructions without deviation. He used to say, "Jerry, hard work never hurt anybody," and "Jerry, you've got to put in an honest day's work for an honest day's pay." I would say, "Yes, sir!" and would comply. To this day, I am still afraid of not complying with his demands on work ethics, even though he passed from this mortal life in 1989. My father, Bob, just like my grandfather, taught me the value of hard work. He served in the military in Korea. My great-grandfather, William Grant, served as an infantryman in World War I.

I am grateful to share my grandfather's middle name, as did his grandfather, Robert L. Mills, a nondenominational preacher, born January 25, 1862 in Fort Scott, Kansas.

The efforts and struggles of my ancestors have raised the economic ship of my family.

A CHANGE IN WORK ETHICS

The current young generation does not appear to have the same work ethic as did their ancestors who struggled through the Great Depression and WWII. The term "hard work" is often an oxymoron to this generation. The current generation seems fixated on personal pleasure and short-term solutions for certain long-term problems.

This generation seems unusually occupied with bad habits and bad behavioral problems, all of which affect their employment. A few of these bad behavioral habits or by-products of bad behavioral habits are as follows:

- Alcoholism

- Divorce

- Watching pornographic websites

- Illegal use of prescription drugs

- Sexually transmitted diseases (AIDS, HIV and the like)

- Use of illegal drugs, such as cocaine, crack, marijuana, etc.

- Sleep deprivation

- Personal financial problems

- Depression

- Obesity

- Chronic fatigue, etc.

No employer wants to know what is going on within the walls of someone else's homes. The thought of such knowledge is repugnant. There are, however, serious economic repercussions to employers for the bad habits of their employees.

I could gather a group of 20 or so employers from any city in the United States and, without exception, this group would likely tell me they are writing checks for the effects of the above behaviors.

If given the opportunity, this group of 20 or so employers would also tell us how they write checks for such behavior. A partial list of their check writing would include some of the following:

- Significant increases in group health insurance costs

- Theft of company assets to support drug habits

- Automobile accidents while on the job

- Increased insurance due to the increased auto accidents

- Sexual harassment lawsuits: male to female, female to male, female to female and male to male

- Fraudulent claims for disability insurance for accidents that did not occur during work hours

- Idle time looking at pornographic websites

- Fraudulent unemployment insurance claims for lawful terminations

- Idle time sending romantic emails or text messages to co-workers

- Downloaded viruses from viewing unauthorized websites

- Idle time spent on MySpace or other non work-related websites

- Theft of intellectual property

- Absenteeism

- High turnover costs

- Increased training costs

- Increased recruitment costs

- Lack of productivity

- Decrease in quality control

- Strife and disharmony among the workforce

- Decreased customer service

- The hiring of additional management to deal with the above problems, etc.

As consumers, you and I are also paying for these costs through increased prices of goods and services or inferior quality for the same. Some of the inferior quality of certain products could possibly cause harm to us or our loved ones.

WHAT CAN BE DONE ABOUT THIS PROBLEM?

Those who plan can often turn a lemon into lemonade. The fact that we need to compete for qualified labor is a good thing in the long run. This means that those who succeed in this area will have a new significant edge over their competitors.

EMPLOYEE MANUAL

Each employer must hire a good attorney and keep an up-to-date employee manual.

This manual must have sections on sexual harassment policies and procedures. The sexual harassment policies and procedures need to be followed to the letter of the law, no exceptions. The business owner must lead by example and must be a champion to those who might be impacted by sexual harassment. Otherwise, litigation, legal fees and moral decay creep into a business.

The employee manual should also contain a drug testing procedure. Prospective employees should be tested for drugs before they are hired. No exceptions should be made for those who test positive for the use of illegal drugs.

The drug-testing procedures should also allow for the legal testing of all employees on a random basis. Laws regarding this matter should be followed, and those who test positive for illegal drugs should be escorted out.

Attorneys should be consulted to help inform you regarding your rights about how employees' use of legal drugs might drive up your company's health insurance costs.

CORE VALUES

I spent a good deal of time in the first chapter of my book, *The Danger Zone, Lost in the Growth* Transition, documenting the need to identify core values in a company. Core values can be defined as:

"The organization's essential and enduring tenets – a small set of general guiding principles; not to be confused with specific cultural or operational practices; not to be compromised for financial gain or short-term expediency."

Some core values that we often see are:

- Honesty and ethics
- Hard work
- Integrity
- Superior customer service
- Constant improvement to the company[31]

You will want to first define the company's core values. You will then want to spend time recruiting and hiring those people who share the company's core values. For example:

Let's say you have a core value of honesty. You hire people who are honest. This honesty is not only in their hearts, but is a part of their being. These people enjoy working with others who share this philosophy.

Let's imagine you then hire a person who is not honest. What is going to happen in this situation? The outcome is predictable; the honest people will feel uncomfortable around the dishonest person. Things will be said behind this person's back such as, "Why do you think the owner hired him?" The dishonest person will try to fit in, but the other employees won't allow this to happen. They may not say anything to the boss (a job security issue), but they will not socialize or trust this person. It would be easier to try to mix water and oil.[32]

Identify the core values of your company. Document them for all to see and start finding people who share them. Skip those who do not comply, regardless of their skill set.

READING

The younger generation seems to have developed a habit of avoiding books. It seems they would rather listen to their iPod, watch videos on websites, go to the movies or be involved in similar such activities.

Mark Twain is credited for saying that a man who does not read good books has no advantage over the man who can't read them.

While growing up, I thought that reading books was a normal process of life. Both of my parents only had a ninth-grade education, but that did not impact my desire to read and to learn. Mrs. Elliott, my sixth grade teacher, offered a silver dollar to the student who read the most books during the nine months of her teaching. The second-place student read about 18 books. I won the silver dollar by reading 100 books, but I did not think that was such a big accomplishment.

There is a great deal of wisdom to be found in books, and it can help us with the employees of today and of the future. For example, James Allen wrote the following in 1910 that might help your employees understand some basic economic laws:

Men do not attract what they want, but what they are.

Not what he wishes and prays for does a man get, but what he justly earns. His wishes and prayers are only gratified and answered when they harmonize with his thoughts and actions.

Men are anxious to improve their circumstances, but are unwilling to improve themselves. They therefore remain bound. Even the man whose sole object is to acquire wealth must be prepared to make great personal sacrifices before he can accomplish his object.

Here is a man who is wretchedly poor. He is extremely anxious that his surroundings and home comforts should be improved. Yet all the time he shirks his work, and considers he is justified in trying to deceive his employer on the ground of the insufficiency of his wages. Such a man does not understand the rudiments of those principles which are the basis of true prosperity. He is not only totally unfitted to rise out of his wretchedness, but is actually attracting to himself a deeper wretchedness by dwelling in, and acting out indolent, deceptive and unmanly thoughts.[33]

Do any current or former employees come to mind upon reading that statement? Perhaps your current and future employees could benefit by reading good books that contain thoughtful applications of basic work ethics and values.

Dale Carnegie published a book in 1944 that has sold more than six million copies. He wrote the following:

Most of us have little trouble "losing ourselves in action" while we have our noses to the grindstone and are doing our day's work. But the hours after work – they are the dangerous ones. Just when we're free to enjoy our own leisure, and ought to be the happiest – that's when the blue devils of worry attack us. That's when we begin to wonder whether we're getting anywhere in life; whether we're in a rut; whether the boss "meant anything" by that remark he made today.

James L. Mursell, professor of education, Teachers College, Columbia, put it very well when he said: "Worry is most apt to ride you ragged not when you are in action, but when the day's work is done. Your imagination can run riot then and bring up all sorts of ridiculous possibilities and magnify each little blunder. At such a time," he concluded, "your mind is like a motor operating without its load. It races and threatens to burn out its bearings or even to tear itself to bits. The remedy for worry is to get completely occupied doing something constructive.[34]

It is not constructive to the mind to watch a lot of television or play video games. Reading books is the remedy to educate the minds of the future generations of people who will work in our companies.

I am not necessarily recommending that the subject matter be limited to business books. One of my favorite diversions from my worries is to read mystery books. I have in my library all of the books written about Sherlock Holmes by Sir Arthur Conan Doyle. I am inspired each time I read books in my library about Abraham Lincoln, George Washington, Benjamin Franklin, Winston Churchill and other world leaders. I am fascinated upon reading books of successful coaches, such as Vince Lombardi or Tom Landry. *As a Man Thinketh*, by James Allen is always uplifting. Zig Ziglar always gives me a boost of energy. The Odyssey of Homer captures the imagination. J.R.R. Tolkien's *Lord of the Rings* trilogy is a great read. And, of course, the scriptures are not to be ignored.

It will take leadership on your part to help your employees read good books. You may need to create rewards or other contests for reading. It may take effort on your part to find good books for your employees to read. The reward will be worth the effort. Hopefully, you will inspire them and help drive out those "blue devils of worry" that Dale Carnegie wrote about in 1944.

You will also begin to notice a nice by-product when your employees read books. Not only will their attitudes improve, but their English and grammar skills will also be enhanced. This skill is imperative to compete for the future, and your company will benefit significantly with these improved employee skills.

COMPETITIVE ADVANTAGE

Mark Twain was wise when he stated that those who do not read books have no "advantage" over those who can't read.

In business, those who read books obtain a business advantage over those who do not.

To compete in the future, the employees of your company need to be better read than the employees of your competitors. You can improve their lives and yours by doing so.

A rising tide does indeed raise all ships. Your company's profits will rise with the improved moral and skills from the well-read employees who share your core values.

CHAPTER 16

Think Like A Buyer to Exit Profitably

The editors of *Strategies Magazine* (www.strategies.com) asked me to write the following article, which was published in their magazine in August 2007.

Benjamin Franklin is credited with the adage, "In this world nothing is certain but death and taxes." That statement is as true today as it was when he wrote it more than 200 years ago. We can add another truism for today's business owners: You will exit your company one day in the future.

Your exit from your company may be planned or unplanned. The exit may bring satisfaction or dissatisfaction to your family. The exit may be to the benefit or detriment of your employees or associates. The exit may bring great financial reward or financial devastation.

The exit may bring fame or shame to your family and friends. The exit may be the continuance or discontinuance of the company you have worked so hard to build and create. The exit may be to the benefit or detriment of your competitors. Regardless of the consequences, you will some day exit your company in one form or another.

"Begin with the End in mind," is a saying made popular by Stephen R. Covey. This is wise advice and should be adhered to by every business owner.

One of the attributes of entrepreneurs is that of being a visionary. It is prudent to begin a vision of a successful exit strategy from your company, since that end is inevitable.

I started my business in 1987. Like many entrepreneurs, in the beginning the End was a tremendous effort to make enough money to feed my family. The End for me was to try to convince future customers they should pay me a fair price for what I was trying to sell.

The End was struggling through the frustrations of being a pioneer in a new industry and the frustration of learning new skills to explain my vision to people that I felt needed my services. In the beginning there were many times that I felt the End might be the failure of my business, my vision and aspirations. I know that many entrepreneurs feel the same way at the outset of their business endeavors.

It is no longer a struggle to meet the financial needs of my family. A business concept that was new and revolutionary in 1987 is now well accepted in our business society and is easy to explain.

It is now time to follow the advice of others and join my fellow entrepreneurs with a new vision of the End with a successful exit strategy. One that is planned, effective and beneficial to everyone. Well, beneficial to everyone except the competition!

What are our options for an exit strategy from our companies? Fortunately, the options are few and easy to comprehend. The central exit strategy themes are as follows:

- Sell the business to a third party

- Sell the business to family members or employees

- Stop the business and convert the assets to cash

- Bankruptcy or other forced liquidations

- Planning for an untimely death

Planning for an untimely death is easy to accomplish through the purchase of adequate life insurance that has a well documented purpose after the need for the insurance.

Personal or family representatives, insurance agents and attorneys can help create a plan that will most likely help you accomplish your key goals with this type of exit strategy. This strategy should begin now and should not be delayed.

THINK LIKE A BUYER

If your exit strategy is to sell the business – whether to a third party, family members or employees – planning how to maximize your income by the sale of your business is essential. Let's assume you wish to sell the company in the future at a fair market value, regardless of who might purchase your business. What, then, are some of the things you can start planning to make this a reality?

Discussing the sale of an entrepreneur's business is a very interesting exercise. Most business owners are adamant about the amount of money they want for the business. They're usually reluctant to accept any outside critique that might conflict with their dollar amount.

Regardless of your feelings about the value of your business, it will most likely be sold using a factor times your company's EBITDA (Earnings before Interest, Taxes, Depreciation and Amortization), averaged over a period of time. The information on this subject is easy to obtain and won't be discussed in this article. Rather, I prefer to try to help you take a step back and look at the big picture regarding the future value of your company.

I'd like to share with you some ideas about the future value of your company in a way that perhaps nobody has suggested.

The easiest way for me to help you with this subject is to have you assume that you are going to buy a business. Let's forget about your business for a while as you consider the following scenario, which will ultimately lead you to a better picture of how to improve the value of your own company.

Pretend that you are the buyer and are interested in purchasing a company. The seller's industry is different from the ones with which you are familiar, but the future of making money with this company looks very promising. The potential purchase of this company meets your goals to diversify your own existing business.

You meet with the owner, talk to some of the customers, meet some of the employees and are excited about the transaction. You have a CVA (Certified Valuation Appraiser) give you a document verifying that the asking price is fair.

You talk about the transaction with your banker. The banker is supportive and agrees to advance money at a reasonable interest rate to help you make the purchase. Everything looks good on paper and feels good in your gut.

Just to be safe, you have a trusted senior-level executive look over the transaction prior to closing the deal. This person also feels good about the purchase, but brings to your attention certain issues that you have not considered so far:

- The customers of the company do business solely based upon the close relationship they have with the company's owner.

- The company's computer hardware is being held together by the owner's brother-in-law on a "fix it when it breaks" approach. Some of the employees complain that the computer and telephone systems crash several times a month. Data is typically lost when the computers crash. The file servers, routers and other company hardware will need to be upgraded or replaced unless the new owner wants to risk a lot of possible down-time with the computer system. It is likely this will cost the new owner six-figures in investment.

- It is possible there will be liabilities for past services to customers. However, the database the seller uses is unreliable, and the estimated warranty issues are not known. You discuss this situation with the current owner. His reply is, "I'll take care of things." You, however, have a nagging feeling in your gut telling you this might lead to possible future relationship problems with the company's customers.

- The procedures to build the goods or deliver the service are not documented in writing. Your advisor raises concern that the knowledge needed to create and deliver goods is merely in the minds of a few key employees. There is no guarantee these people will stay after the sale of the company. In fact, the current owner tells you that a couple of key people will bolt when they hear about the business being sold.

- The selling company has about 50 personal computers, most of which have multiple versions of illegal software. Your advisor tells you that, regardless of the possible issue of software piracy, very few of the computers have the same version of the same software. It is estimated it will cost between $70,000 and $100,000 to correct this problem.

- There is no documentation regarding the intellectual property of the selling company. Doubts are raised by your advisor as to the authority of the selling company to transfer legal rights to these assets. There are also doubts about whether or not the seller legally owns the intellectual property claimed in the sales agreement and Web site.

- There is really no way to verify the accuracy of the numbers presented by the selling company's accounting department. The software is antiquated or corrupted. The conversion of data to a new system and/or the buyer's existing system is doubtful. It is estimated that any conversion or reliability upon the seller's accounting data will take months and a six-figure investment.

- The current owner is working seven days a week and almost 15 hours a day to keep the company going. He has agreed to stay with you for a period of time after the sale to help with the transition. He also wants to take a couple of months off after you give him the check. Your advisor does a little homework and estimates that it might take three people commanding six-figure salaries to replace all of the work being performed by the current owner.

START PLANNING YOUR EXIT NOW

With these facts in mind, what are you going to do now as the potential purchaser of this company? You and I already know the answer: You are going to take the suggested sales price and start subtracting dollars from that amount.

My guess is, from the little information disclosed above, you will subtract a good seven-figure amount from the sales price. Furthermore, you will have justification to go back to the seller to explain why the company is now no longer worth the amount previously discussed, even if your banker has given you the green light to go forward.

With the information you now have, there is nothing in this world that is going to convince you to pay the original sales price. In fact, you may decide that you no longer want to buy the business.

Now, let's consider the potential future sales price of your company. What do you think will happen to the future asking price of your company should a buyer become aware of your infrastructure failures or weaknesses before the close of the transaction?

Well, we know the answer to that question: The buyer will either demand a lower price or will walk away from the deal.

Today is the day to start planning for the sale of your company. Plan to hire key people if you do not have the time to document certain items.

You might need to bring in some senior-level people to organize and document your systems, sometimes known as infrastructure or internal controls. You might consider having certified audits performed on your company's financial statements.

Start asking your key employees to document their activities, with the assumption that someone else might fill their position without doing any damage to the company. Have an independent company take a critical look at your company's computer hardware and software. You might be unpleasantly surprised at the amount of illegal software on your systems.

We can agree that this activity is expensive and time-consuming. It is not nearly as expensive, however, as the missed opportunity for selling your company for a fair price in the future. You have the choice now: Start planning and creating value for your future exit strategy, or be prepared for a future purchaser to have ammunition to lower your suggested sales price. The wise will do the former.

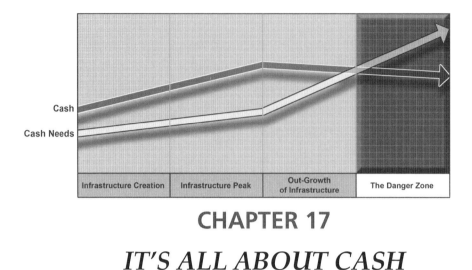

Cash			
Cash Needs			
Infrastructure Creation	Infrastructure Peak	Out-Growth of Infrastructure	The Danger Zone

CHAPTER 17

IT'S ALL ABOUT CASH

The Danger Zone is defined as the situation wherein the cash needs of a company far exceed the available cash. This situation often causes a Chapter 11 bankruptcy filing, liquidation of assets or other time-consuming planning events in order to salvage the company.

A company can never have too much cash. A company can, however, easily run out of cash and get into The Danger Zone. It takes proactive planning to avoid that situation.

You will note that each of the case studies in this book revolves around cash. The selection of these stories and their involvement around cash was not intentional. In business, everything always revolves around cash. I could have replaced all of these stories with others, but the result would have been the same – they would have all revolved around cash. A recap of how these stories revolved around cash is as follows:

Chapter 14:   Ronald used his cash reserves as a down
                payment on a building. He ran out of
                cash and did not pay his state sales
                taxes. The state put a lien on the
                business cash accounts. Ronald had
                to close a business that had been in
                operation for about 35 years.

Cash is king – there is no substitute. Sun Tzu's advice is
very wise; when it comes to cash, plan for everything!

DISTRACTIONS – A RULE OF THUMB

One of the key factors regarding the future cash of your
company will be the use of your time. Recognition is one
of the first steps of stopping a bad habit. The following
graph will help you with this recognition step if you are
spending too much time in Minding activities.

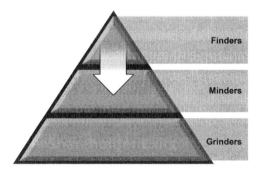

As a rule of thumb, you should not be spending more than 20% of your time in Minding (administrative) activities. You may need outside help if you obtain Minding Cancer as defined in Chapter Three of this book.

As a parallel, cancer often takes outside intervention, such as chemotherapy or other such treatments to kill the cancer. Avoidance of these interventions can lead to death.

Likewise, Minding Cancer often takes outside intervention to help a business owner with the tools necessary to get back into Finding activities. Avoidance of this intervention can cause a company to run out of cash, which eventually can cause the death of the company.

The case studies in this book revealed the deaths of some very long-term companies due to cash depletion. One was a fourth generation, another was a second generation and a third was a 35-year-old business. Death of a company by cash depletion can happen to any company at any time.

The future of your company depends upon your ability to amass and manage cash. Your role as a Finder will be a key component of your company's ability to obtain cash.

BUSINESS ILLUSIONS

Introduced in this book is the concept of how a business owner is similar to a pilot of an airplane. They both take significant risks with their endeavors. Additionally, both of their travels expose them to certain illusions, some of which can be dangerous.

REFERENCE GUIDE

The question, "What can be learned from this story?," is at the end of each of the case-study chapters in this book. There is much knowledge that can be learned from these stories. The cumulative knowledge is insightful. The following is a recap of the lessons learned from each story. The lessons learned are numbered to be used as a reference guide.

Chapter 7 — Suicide

1. A business owner has an opportunity to turn a business around and make a lot of money if there is an investment in getting the company's financial records in order. Good decisions usually happen when a business owner has good information. Bad decisions always occur when an owner has bad financial information.

2. It pays to get rid of incompetent accounting staff that do not use the company's accounting systems properly and/or hide financial information from the owners of the business.

3. Prices can be raised with customers if a logical plan is created, and if the plan is explained to customers in a manner in which the benefit to them is made clear.

4. Talk with someone in the event of a bad situation. Jacob should have talked with George, his attorney and others. He might have been advised that his legal situation was not as serious as was portrayed by law enforcement. Jacob had a first-time misdemeanor offense and could have been

advised how to avoid any serious legal problems. Additionally, George and the rest of us would have let Jacob know that he was loved, respected and would be supported through his ordeal.

5. Follow the advice of medical professionals. Jacob could possibly have avoided this entire situation had he completed his drug rehabilitation and followed the advice of trained medical professionals. He might have kicked his prescription drug habit and lived a happy life.

6. Be careful of prescription drug dependency after surgery. The chemistry of each of our bodies is different. A prescription drug may cause more dependency with one person than it does with another.

7. It is an illusion to assume your estate will carry out your wishes unless those wishes are written in traditional and legal methods. Document your will and get advice from your attorney before the will is completed. Relatives act very funny when it comes to the money of a deceased. Some relatives become greedy and do not care about the wishes for the uses of the money from the deceased family member. Tell your attorney exactly what you want to happen to your company and other assets. Obtain enough legal advice until you are satisfied that your wishes will be followed subsequent to a premature death.

8. Don't ever consider suicide. See someone immediately if you ever have periods where this option is contemplated. Completely ignore this

as an option for exiting any problems. Suicide is an illusion of escape. Get intervention started if you are associated with anyone who is discussing suicide as an escape from his or her problems.

9. Others really care about you. I regret that I never expressed my respect and admiration to Jacob. His former employees and associates still get misty-eyed when they talk about him. They still care deeply about him, even though he has been gone for quite some time. There are likely dozens of people who care about you and your personal well-being but simply do not express such sentiments.

Chapter 8 — Success

10. We live in the greatest country and the greatest times in the history of mankind. It really is possible to start with nothing and become a multimillionaire in this wonderful country.

11. Buyers are typically more interested in operating profits than in gross sales. A business owner should concentrate on increasing EBITDA in order to attract a potential buyer.

12. Business owners should use other people's money - OPM. Banks are in business to make loans and will do so but only if the tax and accounting records of a company are in proper order. Investment in accounting needs to be made in order to obtain bank financing at favorable terms.

13. The professionals we hire should be associated with a company of sufficient size and reputation so

that we will not be harmed if a particular person leaves or stops servicing us. The company should be of sufficient size to allow a fallback person(s) to make sure our needs are covered at all times.

14. An exit strategy that includes a third-party buyer will most likely require financial statements issued by an independent CPA firm. Planning should be made to have a good firm do this work at a reasonable price.

15. Finders should hire the right people who will help get them out of the chains of Minding. Minding activities should be delegated to trusted individuals with the implementation of internal controls to help make sure the trusted employee remains that way. Trust, along with verification, creates a good working environment.

16. The effort to tie the balance sheet information on the tax return to the company's financial statements will greatly assist the company with its efforts with bankers and lenders. It is key to communicate with the preparer of the tax returns. This important function can be accomplished if the corporate records are reported on the accrual basis of accounting, and the tax return is prepared on the cash basis of accounting.

17. It is an illusion to assume a business can keep the sale of a business confidential to all employees during the due-diligence process. This part of the sale of a business is a difficult one and requires much planning to make sure confidences are maintained during the process without too much

business interruption during the due-diligence process.

Chapter 9 — Murder

18. Evil people exist in this world. Some people are evil enough to take the life of a human being in order to satisfy their lust for money and possessions. We need to be cautious and careful with whom we associate. Heed needs to be taken to make sure we, our associates and our valuables are in safe places.

19. We should check to make sure that the named beneficiaries of our life insurance policies are those we want to become beneficiaries in the event of our untimely death.

20. Caution should be used in giving vendors a secured interest in anything involved in our business. Security interests given to vendors grant power to them in ways that may be to our detriment in difficult times.

21. We should have adequate D&O insurance policies. We live in a very litigious society, and caution needs to be given to this area, even if the cost of the insurance premiums seems steep at the time. It is an illusion to think that an owner or officer of a business can operate in perpetuity without being sued for something.

22. Estate planning techniques should be utilized to help minimize income taxes on estate proceeds. Tax avoidance is our legal right as citizens of this great nation. The estate tax field is wide and complex,

but good professionals exist who can help with tax minimization.

23. Actions that we feel are made in secret are sometimes made public. None of us will escape this life without making errors and perhaps without a peccadillo or two. Regardless, we should consider the consequences to our family and friends should those items become public after we have left this mortality.

24. Consider who will run your company in the event of an untimely death. We tend to ignore this uncomfortable subject, but we all came into this life with an expiration date, and those of us who own companies need to make plans accordingly.

25. Nepotism can become a cancer to the business of a deceased business owner. As discussed in Chapter Six of this book, a business owner should adhere to certain prudent business principles when hiring family members.

26. Banks are sometimes loose with their money when a company is perceived to be doing very well. They sometimes will lend unsecured money without personal guarantees. They will, however, quickly clamp down on a business owner if they perceive the business is taking a negative turn.

27. Family members often act in peculiar ways regarding a deceased owner's money or assets. Some family members are not trained or skilled in handling large sums of money in a prudent manner. Additionally, some family members acquire a victim mentality and justify illogical

reasons for believing that the money or possessions of the deceased really belong to them. Family members who control the money of the deceased will not always act in the best interest of minor children or other loved ones who are the deceased's intended beneficiaries. In short, greed sometimes distorts judgment and behavioral decisions, often to the detriment of other family members

Chapter 10 — 8% of the Titanic

28. An exchange of company assets solely for stock options may be an illusion. Cash is king. Beware of companies that make offers to obtain your company's assets for stock or stock options. There may be instances where this economic event is good for you, but cash is often a very good alternative.

29. Seek competent advice before the final sales transaction of your company. Listen to your advisors so you can make an objective decision as to what is best for you and your family.

30. Take advantage of tax laws and tax planning. Seek out the best tax advisors possible and use the tax laws to your benefit.

31. Diversify the lines of business available to your company. Continually look for ways to be less dependent upon one single market in order to prepare for a downturn in the economy or a disaster.

32. Be persistent, as were David and Marla. The 30th U.S. President, Calvin Coolidge, said, *"Nothing in the world can take the place of persistence. Talent will not; nothing is more common than unsuccessful individuals with talent. Genius will not; unrewarded genius is almost a proverb. Education will not; the world is full of educated derelicts. Persistence and determination alone are omnipotent."*

Chapter 11 — A Bank Exit

33. Banks are businesses and may make changes in their short or long term plans as they see shifts in the worldwide economy. Those changes in bank plans may have an impact on your future lending relationships.

34. There are financial institutions that are able to adequately take care of all banking needs. It is an illusion to assume that every bank can take care of all business needs. Risk analysis needs to be considered if 100% of bank lending is with one financial institution.

35. Diversification of the customer base is important. We never want one single customer to become too much of a percentage of total sales. We want to be in a position to continue our business if a customer decides to leave and go elsewhere.

36. Business owners need to know the financial loan covenants that are in their notes payable. Loan covenants in loan documents should be discussed with a financial advisor prior to the signing of the

loan documents. Risk analysis of meeting the loan covenants in the future should be considered and discussed prior to signing the loan documents.

37. Customers sometimes come back after seeing the grass is not so green in other pastures, even the overseas pastures. The laws of supply and demand tend to swing back and forth for entrepreneurs. While it is true that some products can be made cheaper overseas, there sometimes is an issue of quality, delivery and timing.

38. During the good times, bank lending can become habitual. It is often difficult to pass up the money being flaunted by a banker during times of spiraling sales or profits. The additional loans taken, if not carefully analyzed, may haunt a business owner during a downturn in sales, which occurs with most industries.

39. An important banking truism not related to this chapter – it is not uncommon for a business to outgrow a bank. The signs of the outgrowth of a bank are easy to determine if you have a good financial advisor that can read the signals the bank is giving you during the transitional phase.

Chapter 12 — Shareholder Exits

40. Co-owners of a business need to keep an ever-present eye on the financial records of a company. Failure to watch the use of funds by shareholders may result in one party taking more money than agreed upon.

41. Co-owners guilty of taking too much money from the company will not always readily agree to repay the money taken. They have, after all, already shown their lack of character by their theft. They will likely fight very hard to keep their ownership in the company even if they have done harm to another owner.

42. Minority shareholders should not be given stock in a company. Business owners often do this to keep key employees in the company. The minority shareholders who are gifted the stock will rarely appreciate the value of the gift. They have not, after all, made the sacrifices or taken the risks associated with gaining the company's stock. Any buyout of a minority shareholder should be done so with the best interest of the company in mind. An objective third-party appraisal should be prepared. Most importantly, terms should be set by the majority shareholder that will ensure the best working capital situation for the payout, even if the payout is over a long period of time.

43. The past history or longevity of a business has no impact on its ability to survive in the future.

44. Tax laws and other events can cause a company to be severely impacted in terms of its working capital. Adequate working capital must be preserved to be able to weather the storms of such circumstances.

45. Lending institutions are not always there for a company. They are subject to regulators, tax laws and normal business cycles. A company sometimes

needs to spread its debt among several lending institutions.

46. People get greedy when money is involved. One of the oddities in life is, from my perspective, that the people who truly do not understand the difficulty of earning money are usually the ones who become the greediest.

47. The exit of minority shareholders or co-owners can be a very expensive process in terms of both financial and emotional health.

48. It is an illusion to assume Congress will not change tax laws in the future. It is prudent to make decisions based upon the economic viability of the transaction regardless of the tax laws in effect at the time of the decision.

49. If given the opportunity, a business owner should keep all the stock of the company. Other creative financial arrangements should be made in lieu of granting ownership to a minority shareholder.

Chapter 13 — Chapter 11 to Chapter 7

50. Employee theft occurs. Internal controls need to be in place to guard against theft.

51. Someone other than your CPA firm needs to watch over the shoulders of your controller and accounting staff. While nobody can guarantee that theft will not occur in your business, common sense dictates that a monthly visit by a qualified outside party might help deter theft.

52. CPA firms can't be relied upon to uncover theft unless there is a specific engagement letter that specifies the scope and time period for the fraud audit.

53. Most banks will become unfriendly to a business once the numbers begin to slip, regardless of the longevity of the business relationship.

54. Chapter 11 is sometimes a vehicle to be used to give a company time to reorganize and sell its assets and/or intellectual property for a fair-market value.

55. Sexual harassment at any level is against the law. Anyone involved in committing such an act should be prepared for litigation.

56. It is an illusion to operate a business without theft and fraud insurance. A review of the scope and terms of the coverage should be made by the CEO on an annual basis. This is a decision that should not be delegated by the CEO. Advice and consultation should be considered from competent insurance, legal and other advisors.

Chapter 14 — Chapter 11 to Chapter 7

57. Pay federal and state taxes on a timely basis. The government has the power to place liens on cash accounts and is often not reluctant to act quickly against a company. The government is often impartial to issues of a company's ability to make payroll, etc.

58. The government may work with a company that is behind on paying its taxes, but it is an illusion to assume they will always do so or that the work-out plan will always be one that is satisfactory.

59. Do not use working capital to fund the construction of a building. The down payment should come from sources other than working capital.

60. Don't haggle over small items when negotiating the sale of a business. It is not wise to propose changes to a deal after it is written and ready to sign unless one is willing to take the risk of the sale not going through.

61. Be flexible and bend with the competition. Know the trends of the customer and be willing to do what is necessary to beat the competition at their own game.

62. Keep inventory lean. It is better to risk losing a few customers than to carry too much inventory on hand, which will not only use working capital, but might eventually lead to losing more than a few customers.

63. Leave retirement savings alone. That money should be set aside for retirement and should not be used to fund a sinking ship.

64. Secured creditors can't be counted as friends in a Chapter 11 environment. They will take any action needed to protect their secured position, even if the action leads to the eventual closing of a long-term business.

Cash. We Help You Get It.™

APPENDIX

A Word About **B2B CFO**®

The company was formed in 1987.

The firm serves owners of emerging and mid-market companies with revenues up to $75 million that want to increase cash, profitability, sales and company value.

Each partner is a trusted business advisor that creates financial and goal clarity in order to increase cash, profitability, sales and successful exit strategies.

Unlike a full-time or interim CFO, the firm's partners create a long-term professional relationship with a handshake on an affordable as-needed basis. Services are provided on an objective basis by seasoned partners who average 25 years of experience. Partners are supported by thousands of years of collective experience and national partnership resources.

The firm's website is www.b2bcfo.com

NOTE REFERENCES

1. Manage Smarter www.managesmarter.com

2. *Strategies*, August 2007 (www.strategies.com), 8.

3. *Integrity Selling for the 21ˢᵗ Century*, 2.

4. *The Danger Zone, Lost in the Growth Transition*, 21-22.

5. *Integrity Selling for the 21ˢᵗ Century*, 3.

6. *Airplane Crashes*, 29.

7. Wikipedia.

8. *The Naked Pilot, The Human Factor in Aircraft Accidents*, 69-74.

9. Ibid, 74.

10. www.nea.org

11. *Vince, A Personal Biography of Vince Lombardi*, 145.

12. Phrase taught to the author by David Moore, Panamint Group.

13. INC. Magazine, July 2007, 80.

14. *The Millionaire Next Door*, 71.

15. *The Art of War for Executives*, 10, 60.

16. Employee Theft: The Profit Killer (http://retailindustry.about.com/library/uc/uc_case1.htm)

17. *The Danger Zone, Lost in the Growth Transition*, 43.

18. Wikipedia.

19. Apply the 80/20 Rule to Everything in Time and Life Management, Brian Tracy.

20. Bankruptcy by the Numbers, Executive Office of the United States Trustee: http://www.usdoj.gov/ust/eo/public_affairs/articles/docs/abi98febnumbers.pdf

21. Blind Justice, Lady Justice http://www.statue.com/lady-justice-statues.html

22. Wikipedia.

23. http://www.crimelibrary.com/notorious_murders/classics/rick_chance/1.html

24. Wikipedia.

25. The Danger Zone, Lost in the Growth Transition, prelude.

26. Wikipedia.

27. The Arizona Republic, August 25, 2007, A19.

28. http://www.bizjournals.com/phoenix/stories/2004/03/22/story5.html

29. The Danger Zone, Lost in the Growth Transition, 58-59.

30. http://www.bizjournals.com/phoenix/stories/2004/03/22/story5.html

31. The Danger Zone, Lost in the Growth Transition, 7.

32. Ibid, 12.

33. As a Man Thinketh, 22-24.

34. How to Stop Worrying and Start Living, 72.